Navigating the Shadows:

An Integrated Approach to Understanding and Countering Terrorism

by Andrew Weaver

Table of Contents

- Role of International Legal Frameworks and Conventions
- Prospects and Obstacles of Establishing an International Court for Terrorism
- Case Studies

Chapter 21: The Role of Education in Countering Terrorism
- The Power of Education in Preventing Radicalization
- Integrating Counter-terrorism Education into Curricula
- Empowering Teachers and Parents to Recognize Signs of Radicalization
- Challenges and Controversies in Teaching Counter-terrorism
- Case Studies of Educational Initiatives Against Terrorism

Chapter 22: Lessons from History - Case Studies of Resolved Conflicts and Counter-terrorism Successes
- Historical Examples of Conflicts and Terrorism Successfully Resolved
- Strategies, Negotiations, and Policies that led to the Decline of Terrorist Organizations
- Applying Historical Insights to Contemporary Challenges

Chapter 23: Future Trends in Terrorism - Emerging Threats and Responses
- Technological Advancements and Their Impact on Terrorism
- Biological and Chemical Threats: Possibilities and Preparedness
- Space, Cyber, and Quantum Terrorism: Imagining the Unthinkable
- Proactive Approaches: Anticipating and Mitigating Future Threats
- Ethical and Legal Considerations in Addressing Future Terrorism

Conclusion: Navigating the Labyrinth of Terrorism in a Globalized World

Appendices
- Notable Terrorist Attacks Throughout History
- Counter-terrorism Agencies Around the World
- Recommended Reading and Resources

A Note of Thanks to You, the Reader

Introduction

Throughout the annals of human history, certain phenomena persist, adapting and evolving in response to changing times, cultures, and technologies. Terrorism, an ever-present shadow, is one such phenomenon. From ancient zealotry to the digitally-driven extremism of today, acts of terror have continuously morphed in methodology and motivation. As we embark on an exploration of this unsettling yet crucial topic, it is imperative to understand its historical roots, the ever-shifting definitions it has been subjected to, and the immense impact it casts upon societies. Only through this deep understanding can we hope to navigate the challenges posed by terrorism in our increasingly interconnected world.

The Evolution of Terrorism: A Brief Overview

Terrorism's intricate journey across human history reflects its ever-changing face, even at its core—utilizing fear to instigate societal change—has remained unaltered. From the early days, where groups like the Sicarii in Judea and the Hashshashin in Persia utilized targeted violence as a form of communication, the aim has always been to create fear and upset the status quo, driven by deep-seated religious and political beliefs.

Moving into the medieval and early modern eras, acts of terror became more organized. Episodes like the Gunpowder Plot of 1605 highlighted attempts to bring terror to broader audiences, challenging both political and religious authorities.

The 20th century was a watershed moment for terrorism. As the Cold War played out, nations engaged in shadow games, often supporting terrorist groups to weaken rivals. Simultaneously, ethno-nationalist entities like the IRA and ETA leveraged violence in their quests for identity and autonomy. A notable emergence of this era was religious extremism, with jihadist groups targeting global symbols of Western ideologies.

The 21st century opened with the chilling events of 9/11, setting the tone for international counter-terrorism strategies. However, as the world focused on this new brand of terrorism, a digital threat lurked.

Cyberterrorism, characterized by attacks on vital systems and widespread digital propaganda, came to the fore. The rise of social media added another layer to this intricate puzzle, streamlining radicalization, and making the battle against terrorism all the more complicated.

Why Understanding Terrorism Matters

Terrorism is a complex challenge that extends beyond just acts of violence. It is intricately woven with motivations, causes, and effects that permeate societies, creating both obvious and subtle changes. Addressing terrorism requires a comprehensive understanding of its widespread implications.

The political aftermath of a terrorist act often causes shifts in leadership dynamics. Leaders might exploit public sentiment to pass stringent laws, potentially compromising democratic values for perceived security. Political party success can hinge on their stance on terrorism and the perceived efficacy of their counter-terrorism measures. Furthermore, significant terrorist incidents can drive swift policy revisions. Examples include the USA PATRIOT Act following 9/11 and various policy changes in other nations post-terror attacks. Terrorism's main objective is to instill fear, which can mold public perception on numerous issues, ranging from foreign policies to local security initiatives, and even affect interpersonal relationships.

National identities can also be redefined in the wake of terror threats, often solidifying a narrative of "us versus them." This can bolster national unity but at the risk of fostering xenophobia. A major challenge in the post-terror context is the delicate balance between security and freedom. While safeguarding citizens is paramount, there is a risk of infringing on civil liberties in the process. Comprehensive understanding is therefore essential for navigating the complexities of terrorism. Effective counterstrategies need to recognize the historical, sociological, and political contexts from which extremist ideologies emerge, aiming to build societies resilient to extremism.

The human consequences of terrorism are profound. Beyond the immediate physical devastation, there are deeper psychological and social impacts. The direct loss of life is evident, but survivors often grapple with physical and mental scars. Affected communities bear emotional burdens and might suffer disruptions in their social fabric. Societal perceptions and relations can be affected, with certain groups becoming subjects of suspicion and discrimination, thereby potentially exacerbating feelings of disenfranchisement. Addressing these deep-seated impacts requires understanding the mechanisms driving terrorism and establishing support systems for affected individuals.

Economically, terrorism can severely impact sectors like tourism, trade, and investment. Governments might have to reallocate funds to enhance security at the expense of other sectors. Additionally, the social repercussions of terrorism are vast, ranging from increased xenophobia and discrimination to potential erosions in civil liberties.

From a security standpoint, terrorism is a borderless threat, challenging both individual nations and the international community. The interconnected nature of the global landscape means that the effects of a terror act in one region can ripple across the world. National security efforts may involve reevaluating internal threats, addressing infrastructure vulnerabilities, implementing policy changes, and managing civil-military relations. On the global front, concerns range from cross-border terrorism and migration flows to international economic impacts and shifting geopolitical alliances.

The key to effectively countering terrorism lies in a profound understanding of its intricacies. This includes recognizing historical contexts, tracking evolving terrorist methodologies, and being attuned to socio-political landscapes. Equipped with this comprehensive knowledge, nations can devise proactive counter-terrorism strategies. This approach can preempt potential threats, encourage global cooperation, and most importantly, ensure that the pursuit of security does not compromise fundamental democratic values.

With this knowledge, nations can craft counter-terrorism strategies that are not merely reactive but proactive. Such strategies can anticipate potential threats, forge international collaborations, and ensure that in the pursuit of security, the values of freedom and human rights are upheld.

Promoting peace and tolerance is essential in a world where the narrative of terrorism is deeply intertwined with misunderstanding, disenfranchisement, and profound grievances. To move beyond the persistent cycle of violence and retribution, societies must focus not only on countering terrorism but more importantly on fostering peace, understanding, and mutual respect. This involves recognizing and addressing the root causes of terrorism. Many terroristic movements stem from historical conflicts, colonial imprints, or territorial disputes. Acknowledging such historical injustices is pivotal for reconciliation. Similarly, often the regions or communities that feel economically sidelined or socially marginalized become hotbeds for extremist ideologies. Addressing these economic and social disparities can forge a path towards inclusivity.

Furthermore, building bridges through dialogue is crucial. Diplomatic engagements, even with traditionally adversarial groups or states, have the potential to yield unexpected resolutions, diffusing tensions and fostering mutual understanding. Community-level dialogues, where leaders, youth, and influencers converge, can cultivate a unified vision for peace and challenge extremist narratives from within.

Education plays a quintessential role. Reforming curriculums to include lessons on peace, tolerance, and global citizenship can shape a more empathetic and open-minded future generation. Moreover, using both traditional and digital media to share stories that challenge extremist propaganda, like tales of ex-radicals who have turned away from violence, can be impactful.

Another proactive approach involves deradicalization programs. Some nations have set up rehabilitation centers to aid individuals previously involved in extremist activities, focusing on counseling, re-education, and social reintegration. Moreover, with the rise of the internet as a recruitment tool, it is vital to monitor online spaces for signs of radicalization, offering timely support and alternate viewpoints.

Lastly, fostering cultural exchanges can help dissipate misunderstandings. Programs that allow youths from varied backgrounds to immerse themselves in different cultures can challenge preconceived notions and stereotypes. Collaborative art, films, and music projects celebrating diversity can further echo the message of unity, resonating with a wide audience and breaking down prejudice barriers.

Chapter 1:
Historical Roots of Terrorism

Terrorism, while often perceived as a distinctly contemporary menace, actually has ancient antecedents that date back millennia. From the daggers of the Sicarii in Judea to the calculated strikes of the Hashshashin in Persia, the strategic use of violence to instill fear and achieve specific political or ideological goals has been a part of the human story for ages. As societies evolved, so too did the forms and methods of these terror-inducing tactics. The French Revolution, for instance, demonstrated the state's potential to use terror as a means of consolidating power, while the anarchist wave in the late 19th and early 20th centuries highlighted the potential for individuals and small groups to wield disproportionate influence through targeted attacks.

The constants across these varied Instances are the core motivations: to challenge established powers, rectify perceived injustices, or promote particular ideologies. By examining these historical episodes, we can discern certain patterns — the ways in which terror is employed, the typical reactions it provokes, and the long-term effects on societies. Such an exploration not only enriches our understanding of terrorism's deep-seated place in global history but also equips us with the perspective needed to address its contemporary manifestations with a more informed and nuanced approach.

Ancient and Medieval Times

The act of employing fear, intimidation, or violence for achieving political or societal goals is far from a modern invention. Although not explicitly termed as "terrorism" in antiquity, similar activities carried out by smaller groups or organizations have been designed to exert influence by instilling fear and commanding submission from the larger populace.

In the 1st century CE, a radical group known as the Sicarii broke away from the broader Jewish Zealot movement. Named after the Latin word "sica" for a short dagger, the Sicarii became instrumental in shaping early models of politically motivated violence. With Jerusalem as their primary base of operations, they chose assassination as their method to destabilize Roman governance. Their targets were not limited to Roman officials;

Jews perceived to be in collusion with the Romans were also among their victims.

The Sicarii were particularly keen on the setting in which they carried out these violent acts. To maximize the psychological impact of their actions, they strategically chose public spaces for their killings. Marketplaces teeming with people and religious festivals, where the eyes of the community were already focused, became their stages. The visibility served a dual purpose: it sowed terror and emboldened those who were against Roman rule, providing a jarring spectacle that was hard to ignore.

However, the agenda of the Sicarii was not solely political. Their actions were steeped in religious conviction as well. They viewed the Roman occupation as a blasphemous violation of their religious traditions and laws. In doing so, the group intertwined their religious faith with their political activities, setting an early precedent for what future generations would classify as religious terrorism. The blend of deep-rooted religious beliefs with a radical political agenda made them one of the earliest examples of ideologically motivated violence that encompassed both the political and the spiritual.

Moving forward to the 11th century, we encounter a group that refined targeted killings into a high art—the Hashashin, or Assassins. Originating as an offshoot of the Isma'ili sect within Shia Islam, they set up their operations in the formidable mountain fortress of Alamut in present-day Iran. Under the strategic guidance of Hassan-i Sabbah, their operations were not limited to fighting their primary foes, the Sunni Seljuk Turks; they also extended their range to include Christian Crusaders and other political rivals.

What set the Hashashin apart from groups like the Sicarii was their approach to achieving their political and social objectives. Rather than direct, public attacks, they preferred subtlety and subterfuge. Hashashin operatives would often embed themselves within enemy organizations or communities for long durations, gathering crucial intelligence before executing their missions with surgical precision. Their targets were typically influential figures, as they aimed to destabilize and demoralize their enemies through these assassinations.

As we reflect on early instances like the Sicarii and the Hashashin, it is crucial to include them within the evolution of what is now known as 'terrorism.' While the core objective of employing violence to effect political or social change remains constant, the landscape has dramatically transformed. Advances in technology, the scale of operations, and the broader geopolitical implications have all evolved, making the modern manifestation of terrorism far more complex and globally interlinked than its ancient and medieval precursors.

Understanding these ancient and medieval tactics for what they were allows us to better comprehend the historical continuity of employing violence for political or social change. These examples serve as benchmarks that contribute to our understanding of how such tactics have adapted, yet remained an ever-present aspect of human societies through the ages.

Early Modern Period

As we move into the early modern period, the European landscape saw the emergence of anarchism as a potent ideological influence that left a significant imprint on methods of violence aimed at political change. This was a time of significant social, political, and technological transformation, factors that collectively served as a fertile ground for radical ideologies. Among these ideologies, anarchism stood out as a beacon for those disenchanted with the state systems of the time.

One of the groups that best encapsulated this marriage of anarchic ideology with violent tactics were the Russian Nihilists. Originating in the 19th century, they held an extreme form of skepticism toward established social institutions and norms. Their discontent was not limited to philosophical discourse; they took active measures to disrupt the status quo. Armed with their utopian visions of a stateless society, they employed bombings and assassinations as means to an end. Targets usually included high-profile political figures and state institutions, chosen to maximize the impact of their actions.

Similarly, French anarchists, inspired by thinkers like Pierre-Joseph Proudhon and Mikhail Bakunin, were no less committed to realizing their vision of a stateless utopia. They too adopted violent strategies, such as bombings, to shake the foundations of what they viewed as oppressive state systems. Not only were their actions aimed at political figures and institutions, but they also targeted symbols of capitalism and inequality, such as banks, to send a broader message against existing power structures.

The actions of these groups during the early modern period signaled a shift in the methods and philosophies underlying acts of political violence. While their immediate objectives of establishing stateless societies were not achieved, their impact reverberated through history. They set precedents for later forms of organized political violence, including modern terrorism.

Understanding the evolution of political violence, especially through the lens of anarchism during the early modern period, allows for a deeper comprehension of today's complex terrorism landscape. The ideological foundations laid by groups like the Russian Nihilists and French anarchists still echo in various forms of anti-state extremism today, underscoring the enduring and evolving nature of politically-motivated violence.

The 20th Century: A Century of Ideological Extremes

The 20th century stands as a grim monument to the escalation and diversification of ideologically-motivated violence. Terrorism, now a global phenomenon, found fertile ground in a variety of socio-political landscapes. Nationalist, Marxist, and ethno-nationalist ideologies were some of the prominent driving forces behind acts of terrorism during this time. The century served as a vivid illustration of how political violence could transcend borders and infiltrate diverse cultures and societies.

One of the most prominent nationalist movements that resorted to terrorism was the Irish Republican Army (IRA). Rooted in a desire for Irish independence from British rule, the IRA engaged in a protracted campaign of bombings, kidnappings, and assassinations. Their violent tactics became emblematic of the lengths to which nationalist groups would go to achieve their political objectives, setting a precedent for similar movements worldwide.

Equally fervent in their ideological commitment were the Marxist groups, with Italy's Red Brigades standing out as a prime example. Driven by their interpretation of Marxist-Leninist principles, they targeted politicians, judges, and business leaders in a quest to topple what they perceived to be a corrupt capitalistic system. Their actions added another layer of complexity to the multifaceted phenomenon of modern terrorism.

The 20th century also brought to light the horrifying potential of ethno-nationalist conflicts, with the genocide between the Hutus and Tutsis in Rwanda serving as a case in point. At its' core, this conflict was not terrorism in the conventional sense, but it displayed how ideological extremes could fuel mass violence and atrocities. The Rwandan genocide illustrated that ideological fanaticism could lead to acts of indescribable brutality.

While the early part of the century was largely dominated by secular ideologies, the latter half saw a significant upswing in religiously-motivated terrorism. Groups like Hezbollah in Lebanon, the Tamil Tigers in Sri Lanka, and various Islamist extremist organizations came to prominence. These groups melded religious fervor with political aims, generating a new and potent form of terrorism that began to play an increasingly significant role on the global stage.

The 20th century serves as a sobering testament to the range and scope of ideologically-driven violence. The era saw the evolution of terrorism from localized movements to complex global networks. Understanding the multifarious motivations behind these acts is crucial for comprehending—and countering—the terrorism we encounter today.

The Age of Global Terrorism

As the world crossed the threshold into the 21st century, terrorism underwent a radical transformation, manifesting itself as a global menace with far-reaching implications. Gone were the days when acts of terrorism were mainly localized or confined to a specific nation or region. Events like the September 11 attacks in the United States, the Madrid train bombings, and the London subway bombings served as harrowing markers of this new era. These incidents captured the attention of the world, triggering collective anxiety and necessitating an international approach to counter-terrorism.

The September 11 attacks in 2001 were a watershed moment, altering not just U.S. foreign and domestic policy but also shaping global counter-terrorism strategies. Carried out by al-Qaeda, these coordinated suicide attacks on American soil demonstrated the lengths to which modern terrorist organizations could go to inflict maximum damage and casualties. The audacity and scale of the attacks prompted an immediate, wide-ranging international response, spearheaded by the U.S. but involving dozens of nations.

Following closely on the heels of 9/11, Europe became a theater of significant terrorist activity with attacks in Madrid in 2004 and London in 2005. These incidents demonstrated that no region was insulated from the threat of terrorism. European nations subsequently bolstered their internal security measures, and counter-terrorism became a top agenda item for the European Union.

As the world grappled with the evolving threat, the emergence of the Islamic State of Iraq and Syria (ISIS) added a new and horrific dimension to global terrorism. Unlike previous groups, ISIS established territorial control over significant portions of Iraq and Syria and utilized sophisticated propaganda tools, mainly through the internet, to recruit fighters from around the world. Their acts of extreme brutality, often broadcast for global consumption, marked a grim evolution in terrorist tactics.

The advent of the internet has acted as a force multiplier for terrorist activities. Not only has it served as a recruitment tool, but it has also provided a platform for fundraising, radicalization, and even remote plotting. Cyber-terrorism is now a real and growing concern. Consequently, cybersecurity measures are increasingly considered a crucial part of international counter-terrorism efforts.

The ubiquity and scale of modern terrorism have prompted unprecedented levels of international cooperation. Initiatives now span multiple continents and involve a range of actors, from national governments to intergovernmental organizations like the North Atlantic Treaty Organization (NATO) and the United Nations (UN). The world has come to realize that combating terrorism is a shared responsibility requiring coordinated global action.

The 21st century has defined itself as an age of global terrorism, stretching the boundaries of what societies thought possible, both in terms of the level of organization among terrorist groups and the sheer scale of violence. This new era has forced a collective reckoning, requiring a unified and comprehensive international strategy to mitigate the ever-evolving threat.

State-Sponsored Terrorism a Geopolitical Strategy

State-sponsored terrorism is not a new phenomenon; its roots can be traced back to various points in history when governments sought to gain the upper hand against rivals or to secure their own regimes. During the Cold War, for example, both the United States and the Soviet Union were accused of supporting rebel groups or paramilitaries to influence third-world countries. Sponsorship often involved financial aid, military training, and provision of arms, turning these groups into proxies that could undertake activities that states could not directly engage in due to international law or public opinion.

When states engage in sponsorship, they usually maintain a level of plausible deniability, aiming to keep their involvement obscured or ambiguous. This deniability allows them to reap the benefits of destabilizing an adversary or extending their own influence while avoiding the diplomatic or military repercussions that could result from overt actions.

The tapestry of terrorism is intricate and complex, woven together by threads of historical events, ideologies, and the evolving nature of human conflict. The historical roots of terrorism are deep and varied, shaped by countless actors and circumstances over the years. Understanding this history is not just an academic exercise but a critical endeavor that can shed light on the motivations and methods of contemporary terrorist groups, thereby helping to formulate more effective counter-terrorism strategies.

Understanding terrorism in its historical context allows us to see it not as an isolated or modern phenomenon but as a form of political violence that has been employed throughout human history. Such a perspective can serve as a foundation for more effective counter-terrorism policies, which not only seek to address immediate threats but also understand the deeper, underlying causes of terrorism.

Chapter 2:
The Psychology of Terrorism

Decoding the motivations and mental states behind acts of terrorism is not just an academic exercise; it is an urgent necessity. The psychological architecture of terrorism offers invaluable insights into how and why individuals and groups turn toward violent extremism. Understanding these factors is crucial for various stakeholders, from policymakers and law enforcement agencies to psychologists and community leaders, as it can inform more effective counter-terrorism strategies.

The psychological underpinnings of terrorism are intricate and multifaceted, encompassing a range of influences from personal inclinations and group ideologies to societal circumstances and specific situational factors. Given the interplay of these various elements, each act of terrorism emerges as a distinct manifestation of this complexity, making the occurrence challenging to dissect and comprehend.

While some terrorists act based on personal motivations—such as revenge, the need for recognition, or the quest for a sense of purpose— others are driven by collective ideologies. This could range from religious dogmas and extremist political views to racial or ethnic supremacism. Understanding the interplay between individual psychological needs and collective ideologies can provide a more comprehensive picture of why terrorists do what they do.

Another important aspect to consider is the emotional state of individuals involved in acts of terrorism. Anger, frustration, humiliation, and fear are a few of the emotions that can fuel extremist actions. However, these emotional triggers are often rationalized through ideological frameworks, which provide a 'moral' or 'logical' basis for acts that are fundamentally irrational and violent.

Lastly, terrorism does not happen in a vacuum. It is fostered by an ecosystem that may include social networks, communities, and even nations that either directly or indirectly support the radical beliefs leading to terrorism. Within these ecosystems, individuals or groups receive not just ideological but also logistical support for their extremist activities.

Motivations: Ideology, Religion, and Politics

Ideology is a complex lens through which individuals interpret the world, acting as both the emotional and intellectual catalyst for extremist actions. In the realm of terrorism, ideologies can vary widely, encompassing beliefs from religious fundamentalism to political extremism and even deep-seated prejudices around race or ethnicity. Such ideologies offer an unambiguous moral framework that becomes intoxicating for the believer. It is a clarifying force that defines who is part of the 'in-group' and who belongs to the 'out-group,' what is right and what is wrong. This potent sense of certainty can embolden individuals to commit violent acts under the conviction that they are contributing to a noble cause or higher power.

Within this ideological commitment, violence is often rationalized as a necessary evil to attain a greater good. It shifts from being seen as an immoral act to becoming a justifiable tool in service of a larger cause. This rationalization is apparent across various ideological landscapes, be it political movements that term such violence as 'revolutionary,' or religious extremes where it is seen as a 'divine' command. The ideology thus serves not just as a justification but also as a powerful recruitment tool. Extremist groups target individuals who already have some sympathetic beliefs and then offer a more radicalized perspective, often facilitated by charismatic leadership and the dynamics of a tightly-knit community that serves to reinforce these beliefs.

While one might think of ideology as a purely intellectual construct, it has deep psychological and emotional resonances as well. For people who feel marginalized or disenfranchised, the extremist ideology offers more than just beliefs; it offers a sense of purpose, a community, and even a hero's narrative. It can empower individuals to act against what they perceive as systemic injustices, making them active players in a story where they can make a 'difference.'

However, the very strength of ideology is also its weakness: its often absolutist nature. When an ideology is so rigid that it allows for no questions or compromises, it can foster a black-and-white worldview. In such a framework, anyone outside the ideological belief system becomes not just an outsider but an enemy deserving of eradication. This can make it psychologically easier to commit acts of violence against them. This absolutism is not static; people can and do change their beliefs based on new experiences, information, or other influences, offering pathways for intervention and deradicalization.

Religious extremism serves as another potent motivator for terrorist actions. For some individuals engaged in such acts, the belief that their violent deeds are not just condoned but actually mandated by a higher power provides a powerful moral framework. This perspective reframes acts of terror, turning them from immoral violence into something they perceive as spiritually obligatory. The belief that these acts are divinely sanctioned can therefore imbue these individuals with a sense of moral certitude that can be both empowering and dangerous.

Within this divinely inspired framework, violence becomes not just permissible but a form of sacred duty, a way to attain spiritual rewards or to fight against what is perceived as evil or corrupt. This aspect of religious extremism complicates efforts to counteract terrorism, as combatting the ideology involves challenging deeply-held spiritual beliefs, which are often more resistant to change compared to secular ideologies.

This sort of religious motivation also creates a unique form of community among like-minded individuals. There is a spiritual brotherhood or sisterhood that emerges, creating a support network that further reinforces the belief that these acts of terror are part of a divinely ordained mission. The community aspect can make the individual's commitment to the cause even more resolute, thereby making intervention and deradicalization much more challenging. Therefore, understanding the role of religious beliefs in motivating terrorism is crucial for any comprehensive strategy aimed at prevention and deradicalization.

Additionally, political motivations frequently act as a driving force for terrorist activities, sometimes overlapping with ideological or religious convictions, but often standing alone as well. For instance, feelings of nationalism can fuel desires for a homeland that, in the minds of some, justifies the use of violent tactics. The quest for political independence can inspire separatist movements that resort to acts of terror as a means to achieve their ends.

Similarly, discontentment with the existing political environment can serve as a catalyst for radicalization. This can take the form of perceived infringements on rights, allegations of governmental malfeasance, or the state's inability to fulfill basic civic needs. When individuals believe that conventional democratic avenues like voting or nonviolent demonstrations are inadequate for redressing their complaints, they may rationalize the use of violence as an alternative means of political expression.

Therefore, it is essential to understand the complex landscape of political motivations behind terrorism, as these are often deeply rooted in historical and socio-political contexts. Each form of political motivation offers its own set of challenges for prevention and deradicalization, which underscores the need for a nuanced approach in tackling the various kinds of extremism. Fully grasping the impact of political motivations not only enriches our understanding of why terrorism occurs but also informs more effective counter-terrorism strategies.

The Mind of a Terrorist: Radicalization Processes

The pathway to radicalization often commences with initial contact to extremist content or influential figures advocating for violent ideologies. These initial encounters can happen in various settings, ranging from online platforms to community gatherings, and they can act as catalysts for further exploration into extremist thought. It is not a one-size-fits-all process; different people are influenced in different ways and through different channels, but the end result can be the same: a commitment to extremist actions.

Individuals who are particularly susceptible to these influences often deal with personal or societal challenges that make them more receptive to extremist messaging. This vulnerability could stem from a range of issues, such as emotional trauma, social marginalization, or economic hardship. Faced with these challenges, they may find the simple, black-and-white solutions offered by extremist ideologies appealing. The sense of belonging and purpose provided by extremist groups can offer a temporary relief from their daily struggles, acting as a magnet that pulls them further down the path of radicalization. In essence, the intertwining elements of exposure and vulnerability form a complex web that can trap individuals and lead them towards extremism.

The gradual acceptance of extremist beliefs often happens as individuals encounter more and more ideological material and engage with people who share those views. Over time, the constant exposure and social reinforcement make the extremist ideology become an integral part of their personal belief system. This ideological solidification is often a mutual process; as the individual commits to the group's ideology, the group, in turn, provides a community that reinforces that individual's newly adopted beliefs.

It is not just about accepting a set of ideas; it is about joining a community that shares those ideas and offers social validation for them. The sense of community, combined with the ideological commitment, can be a potent mix, making the person feel more invested in the extremist cause. In such a setting, the lines between individual and collective beliefs blur, making it increasingly difficult for the person to distinguish their own thoughts from the group's views.

Understanding the process of ideological adoption or indoctrination is essential for grasping the psychological complexities that fuel extremism. It can also provide a roadmap for interventions aimed at reversing or halting the process of radicalization.

In the end, there is a pivotal moment when an individual or group makes the psychological leap from merely holding extremist beliefs to actually acting on them. This transition represents a significant mental shift. It is one thing to harbor extreme opinions or engage in hate speech, but it is quite another to carry out an act of terrorism. The crossing of this psychological boundary is often the result of a complex interplay of factors, including ideological conviction, emotional triggers, and social pressures.

The act of planning and executing a terrorist action is not an impulsive decision but the culmination of ideological indoctrination, emotional engagement, and often, group dynamics that validate and reinforce an extremist belief system. By the time the act is carried out, the individual or group has usually developed a robust rationalization that situates the act of violence within a larger narrative of struggle or resistance. This narrative helps to mitigate any cognitive dissonance that might arise from committing violent acts that society condemns but their belief system glorifies.

Understanding this critical transition from belief to action can provide valuable insights for counter-terrorism efforts. Recognizing the psychological mechanisms at play can help in the development of interventions aimed at preventing the progression to violent actions. Whether through community-based programs, law enforcement strategies, or psychological interventions, grasping the complexities of this final stage of radicalization is crucial for both preventing terrorism and deradicalizing those already involved in extremist activities.

Root Causes of Terrorism - Understanding the Underlying Factors

Socio-economic imbalances like poverty, joblessness, and social inequality are often cited as fertile grounds where terrorism can take root. While not direct instigators of terrorism themselves, these conditions create a climate where extremist ideas can gain traction. Individuals who are disenfranchised or marginalized in their communities may find the simple solutions offered by extremist ideologies to be particularly compelling. The promise of not just a purpose, but perhaps also material or social gains, can make these ideologies highly attractive.

In societies marked by stark social and economic disparities, the feelings of humiliation, alienation, or injustice are heightened. These emotions can become powerful catalysts that drive people toward extremist groups, which often offer not just a radical ideological solution, but also a sense of community and individual significance. The narrative provided by these groups often frames the individual's personal struggles as part of a larger battle, imbuing their life with meaning and contributing to the rationalization of violence as a necessary course of action.

Moreover, radical organizations frequently take advantage of these socio-economic situations to attract fresh recruits. They tap into people's frustrations and offer them a sense of community or mission that may be lacking in their current circumstances. Hence, tackling these root socio-economic issues could be a vital strategy in curbing the rise of extremist ideologies. Enhancing quality of life, creating employment opportunities, and rectifying systemic disparities may diminish the allure of radical belief systems, hindering their ability to establish a strong base of support.

The feeling of being unjustly treated or politically marginalized frequently acts as a mechanism for radical actions. When people or communities believe their concerns are being ignored or dismissed by those in authority, they may grow more receptive to extremist viewpoints. This sense of grievance can develop into a compelling storyline that rationalizes resorting to extreme measures as a way to redress these perceived wrongs.

Moreover, disenfranchisement from mainstream politics can create a vacuum that extremist ideologies are all too willing to fill. When people feel they have no stake in the existing political system, or that the system itself is rigged against them, they may seek alternative routes for political expression. In such cases, the allure of extremist groups that promise to overthrow or disrupt the established order can become increasingly compelling.

This sense of grievance against a ruling entity can be leveraged by extremist groups to recruit and radicalize individuals. They offer an avenue for these individuals to express their frustrations and take 'concrete' action against what they perceive as a corrupt or unjust system. In the eyes of the recruit, the extremist cause can seem like a fight for justice or freedom, which can in turn make it easier to rationalize violent actions as a means to a 'noble' end.

In summary, the underlying feeling of having been politically sidelined or wronged can act as a spark for embracing extremist actions. Addressing such grievances and fostering political inclusivity can thus serve as a countermeasure to diminish the appeal of extremist ideologies.

Personal issues can serve as potent reasoning for pushing individuals towards extremist behaviors. Among these issues are fundamental psychological needs for identity and belonging. When people feel disconnected or alienated, the allure of a group that offers a strong sense of community and purpose can be highly seductive. Extremist groups often offer not just a sense of belonging but also a clear-cut identity that stands in opposition to perceived enemies or societal values, turning them into attractive havens for those who feel out of place in their current circumstances.

Beyond the quest for identity and belonging, the desire for revenge can be another driver towards extremism. People who have suffered personal or perceived collective injustices may harbor intense feelings of anger and a desire for retribution. In such emotional states, the line between justice and revenge can blur, making it easier to rationalize extreme actions. Extremist groups can channel these emotions into violent acts, presenting them as a form of justified vengeance against those who have supposedly wronged the individual or their community.

It is important to recognize that individual factors like the quest for identity or the urge for revenge often intersect intricately with wider social, economic, and political dynamics. For example, the search for a sense of belonging can intensify when set against a backdrop of social isolation or political marginalization. Likewise, the impulse for vengeance may escalate in the midst of prevailing social discord or global tensions. Therefore, although these elements may start as personal motivations, they commonly combine into broader systemic challenges, feeding into a recursive cycle of extremism and aggression.

Understanding these intricate psychological and identity-related factors is crucial for devising effective strategies to counter radicalization and extremism. Whether it is through community programs aimed at fostering a sense of belonging or psychological interventions to address issues like anger and the need for revenge, addressing these underlying factors can be a critical component in preventing the escalation from grievance to violent action.

Cultural norms and the broader ideological fabric of a society can also play a significant role in shaping an individual's views and behaviors, sometimes fueling or tempering extremist tendencies. In some cultures, for instance, authoritarian or patriarchal values may reinforce attitudes that predispose people to extremist ideologies. On the other side, societies that prioritize pluralism and tolerance might make it less likely for extremist ideologies to take root among individuals.

Societal ideologies also function as a prism through which individuals interpret the world around them. Whether it is a belief system that emphasizes individual liberties or collectivist values, these ideological frameworks shape the way people understand issues like justice, equality, and authority. This becomes especially critical in polarized environments, where contrasting ideologies can heighten tensions and aggravate divisions, sometimes serving as a precursor to extremist views.

It is crucial to understand that culture and ideology are not fixed; they can evolve due to various influences such as political shifts, economic changes, and social trends. These dynamic factors often interact with elements like personal psychology and socio-economic status, creating a multi-layered environment that can either inhibit or accelerate the spread of extremism.

Understanding the impact of cultural and ideological drivers in either mitigating or exacerbating tendencies toward extremism is vital for creating effective prevention strategies. It is not simply about identifying the 'bad' ideologies but about understanding how various cultural norms and societal beliefs interact with individual psychology and broader social conditions. Therefore, any attempt to address extremism must consider the cultural and ideological context in which it emerges, to devise a complete approach that tackles the root causes.

The psychology of terrorism is a compilation of factors, ranging from individual motivations to broader social and political contexts. While no single understanding can entirely prevent terrorism, grasping its psychological bedrocks is crucial for formulating effective counter-terrorism strategies. By investigating the motivations that drive terrorism, we equip policymakers, law enforcement, and social experts with the tools to create interventions and policies aimed at addressing the root causes. This not only reduces the attractiveness of extremist ideologies but also dismantles the psychological frameworks that encourage and perpetuate terrorist activities.

**Chapter 3:
Root Causes of Terrorism - Understanding the Underlying Factors**

While the immediate imagery evoked by terrorism often paints a vivid tableau of destruction, chaos, and visceral pain, the undercurrents that propel individuals or groups toward such extreme actions are seldom straightforward or easily discernible. Beneath the visible surface of these acts lies a labyrinthine maze of socio-economic, political, and psychological drivers.

To navigate this intricate network, one must delve deeper than the mere act itself and venture into the murkier territories of societal disparities, political disenfranchisement, and deeply rooted psychological traumas. Socio-economic factors, ranging from unemployment, poverty, to lack of education, can create an environment rife for radical ideologies to take root. Coupled with political factors, such as oppressive regimes, foreign interventions, or longstanding territorial disputes, individuals may find themselves marginalized, their voices silenced, and their identities in crisis. This potent mix can trigger profound psychological repercussions, leading to feelings of alienation, humiliation, or a desire for revenge. In such fertile grounds, extremist ideologies may not just thrive, but they can seem like the only beacon of hope or avenue of expression.

By diligently unpicking this intricate tapestry, societies can gain a richer, multi-dimensional insight into the genesis of terror. It is through this understanding, by identifying and addressing the root causes, that societies might not just respond to, but also preemptively stymie the tendrils of terrorism. Offering more inclusive platforms, socio-economic upliftment, political representation, and psychological support can illuminate alternative pathways, veering potential radicals away from the abyss of extremism and towards avenues of constructive engagement and coexistence.

Socio-economic Disparities

Socio-economic disparities, a complicated and deep-seated issue in many societies, frequently reveal themselves in diverse and often subtle ways. Their pervasive influence has the uncanny ability to sculpt the very essence of our collective social fabric, pushing individuals into directions and choices they may never have envisioned for themselves under different circumstances.

To take a closer look, consider the profound impacts of economic deprivation, where the stark, often grim reality becomes undeniably clear. It is a world where communities, entire generations, or isolated individuals are perpetually marginalized. Continually denied access to essential resources, or tethered to an environment barren of job opportunities, they find themselves ensnared in the cruel grips of cyclical poverty. And as days turn into years, a profound sense of despair, disenfranchisement, and disillusionment starts to take root.

This disturbing scenario extends beyond just the tangible lack of material assets. At its core, it is about the gradual, painful erosion of hope, of personal dignity, and of visions for a brighter and more prosperous future. And when one starts to discern that these economic deprivations are not mere unlucky twists of fate but rather calculated, and sometimes deliberate, acts of systematic oppression perpetuated by more dominant power structures, the scenario grows even darker.

Such fertile grounds, tainted with resentment and feelings of powerlessness, become the perfect breeding places for radical ideologies. In the midst of the shadows cast by economic disparity, extremist factions often rise, presenting themselves not just as temporary financial lifelines but as the beacon of hope. They offer not only the allure of financial respite but also a renewed sense of purpose, a reclaimed identity, and a burning desire for retaliation against those who, in their eyes, are the very oppressors that brought them to this state of despair.

Expanding on the theme of educational disparities, it is critical to understand that the absence or insufficiency of quality, comprehensive education can severely undermine the pillars of a prosperous society. Education, in its essence, is not merely a process of imparting knowledge; it serves as a lighthouse, guiding individuals by empowering their minds, nurturing their innate capacities, instilling in them the virtues of critical thinking, and equipping them with tools for discernment and informed decision-making.

However, when societies falter in providing these fundamental educational pathways, or when they deliver subpar, underfunded, and disjointed educational experiences, it invariably creates a vast void. This educational vacuum is not just an empty space—it is a dangerous chasm, a fertile ground where misinformation, prejudice, and dogma find their way, thriving unchecked and unchallenged.

Astute and opportunistic extremist groups, ever watchful for such vulnerabilities, can swiftly position themselves in the role of educators or mentors. Yet, the brand of 'education' they provide often comes with ulterior motives. It is rarely, if ever, an unbiased, broad-based learning experience. Instead, while they might impart certain valuable skills or rudimentary knowledge, their teachings are frequently interwoven with heavy ideological slants. This strategy effectively turns educational settings into factories that churn out young, impressionable minds, transformed into ardent foot soldiers championing their cause.

As these individuals mature, the extremist teachings they have absorbed often solidify, becoming the dominant, unyielding lens, through which they interpret the world. This skewed perspective obscures alternative viewpoints, diverse narratives, and the rich tapestry of human thought and culture.

Hence, when we scrutinize the convergence of economic deprivation with these educational chasms, the implications are staggering. It is not merely about individual futures being at risk; it is the very fabric of societal cohesion that is in peril. The harmonious coexistence of diverse groups, the free exchange of ideas, and the growth of enlightened, progressive societies—all stand jeopardized. Recognizing this, there is a palpable urgency for society, policymakers, and global leaders to engineer proactive, comprehensive, and holistic interventions. These solutions must not only bridge these alarming gaps but also staunchly counteract the insidious forces seeking to exploit them.

Political Grievances

Political grievances, especially those deeply rooted in profound feelings of marginalization and discrimination, can profoundly influence the trajectories of individuals and entire communities. It is an irrefutable fact that populations or specific groups that perceive themselves as victims of systemic marginalization or are blatantly sidelined by state policies or broader societal norms experience a growing chasm of disenfranchisement. This feeling is not merely transient discontent; it is a deep-seated sense of being persistently pushed to the edges of societal consideration, rendered voiceless in the very spaces they inhabit.

Amid such oppressive circumstances, these groups often grapple with a sense of invisibility, feeling that their voices remain unheard, their concerns dismissed, and their aspirations stifled in the grander tapestry of national or global discourse. This exclusion from mainstream dialogues, coupled with consistent injustice, can amplify feelings of despair and frustration. As these feelings brew and intensify, some segments within these marginalized communities, perhaps those most disenfranchised or radicalized, might contemplate and eventually resort to extreme measures, such as terrorism.

It is imperative to understand that resorting to such extreme actions is rarely, if ever, a first choice. More often than not, it is a cry of desperation, an act born out of the perceived need to shake the status quo, to be noticed, and to have their grievances acknowledged on a platform that cannot be ignored. The objective is not solely to express dissent; it is an attempt to magnify their issues, making them impossible to overlook by the international community, national entities, policymakers, and the public at large.

While these extremist actions do not, and should not, represent the views or methods endorsed by the broader community from which these factions arise, their emergence highlights a crucial flaw in societal structures. It pinpoints areas where dialogue is lacking, representation is minimal, and integration is incomplete. This web of complexities emphasizes the pressing need for governments and societies to prioritize inclusive governance, proactive outreach, and the genuine redressal of grievances. In doing so, the aim should be to create an environment where every individual feels acknowledged, understood, and valued, thereby negating any perceived necessity for radical or violent expressions of dissent.

The Colonial Era, with its vast web of domination and subjugation, left indelible imprints on many regions of the world. Long after the departure of colonial powers, the regions they once ruled still grapple with a complicated legacy that touches upon social, economic, political, and cultural dimensions. One of the most profound and, often, destabilizing remnants of this era is the rise of radical movements that, in many ways, find their genesis in the deep-seated grievances of historical injustices.

Colonial rulers frequently employed tactics of divide and rule, exacerbating existing ethnic or religious differences, and often redrawing borders with little regard for indigenous cultures and historical territories. Such actions often sowed the seeds of discord, the repercussions of which are still felt in contemporary geopolitical conflicts. For example, the 1947 Partition of India marked the redrawing of political boundaries and the redistribution of resources following the end of British colonial rule in the Indian subcontinent, leading to the establishment of India and Pakistan. This significant event triggered a massive migration between the two new nations and resulted in substantial loss of life.

Post-colonial states, while gaining sovereignty, inherited fractured societies, artificial borders, and deeply entrenched hierarchies that were favorable to the colonizers. As these nascent nations sought to carve out a sense of identity and purpose, the painful memories of exploitation, cultural erosion, and displacement became potent rallying cries for movements seeking redressal and justice.

Many radical groups today anchor their ideologies in these historical wounds. They present themselves as the torchbearers of resistance against past oppressions, often romanticizing the pre-colonial era and promising a return to perceived lost glories. While their methods and ideologies may be extreme, their appeal often lies in evoking shared memories of colonial subjugation. For nations and global communities aiming to counteract such radicalism, understanding this deeply rooted historical context is essential. Only by acknowledging the past, addressing the valid grievances, and working towards a future built on mutual respect and understanding, can the shadows of colonialism truly be dispelled.

Psychological and Identity Factors

The human psyche is a complex tapestry of emotions, beliefs, and needs, with one of its most profound yearnings being the quest for identity and belonging. Throughout our lives, particularly during formative years and times of upheaval, this search becomes paramount, shaping our perceptions, actions, and affiliations. Amidst the tumult of such existential pursuits, extremist ideologies can emerge as a beacon, promising clarity, purpose, and a community that understands and embraces one's struggles.

Individuals, especially those on the margins or feeling disenfranchised, can find in these ideologies a refuge from their feelings of alienation and uncertainty. In a world that might seem increasingly fragmented and impersonal, extremist groups offer a narrative that seemingly makes sense of the chaos, providing both an external 'other' to rally against and a clear set of principles to adhere to. The allure of such a black-and-white worldview, coupled with the promise of camaraderie, can be deeply enticing.

This intertwining of psychological needs and extremist ideologies is not just an individual phenomenon. It reflects broader societal issues — from systemic inequalities and lack of inclusive spaces to the challenges of multiculturalism and rapid globalization. Addressing the root of this allure necessitates a deep understanding of human psychology and the social environments that breed feelings of alienation. For societies and communities, it is imperative to create spaces where diverse identities can coexist, thrive, and engage in constructive dialogues, ensuring that the search for identity leads to bridges, not barricades.

At the crossroads of personal trauma and societal tensions lies a potent catalyst for radicalization: personal grievances. Every individual, as they journey through life, accumulates experiences — some uplifting, others deeply scarring. For those who have faced traumatic events, harbored personal vendettas, or perceived injustices directly aimed at them, the world can often seem an arena of relentless hostility. Such personal turmoil, when not addressed or reconciled, can create fissures in one's psyche, making them susceptible to ideologies that promise justice, vengeance, or an avenue to voice their anguish.

The journey from personal grievances to radicalization is not linear, nor is it the same for everyone. It is a confluence of multiple factors — the intensity of the trauma, the individual's coping mechanisms, the environment they are in, and the influences to which they are exposed. In some instances, a singular event, like the loss of a loved one in a conflict, can become the defining moment, propelling them toward extremism. For others, it might be a series of perceived slights and injustices accumulating over time, gradually eroding their trust in mainstream systems and values.

Radical groups often capitalize on these personal narratives of suffering, offering not just empathy but also a clear enemy and a promise of retribution. The seductive allure of being part of a larger cause, where one's personal pain is validated and amplified, can be overpowering. Addressing this requires a multi-pronged approach: from providing trauma counseling and support networks to ensuring that legitimate grievances find a platform for redressal within society. Without this, the cycle of personal pain transforming into broader societal discord will continue unabated.

Cultural and Ideological Drivers

Religion, in its purest form, stands as a beacon of hope, morality, and solace for billions worldwide. It offers spiritual guidance, a moral compass, and a sense of community. Yet, within the vast tapestry of beliefs and interpretations, lie extremist factions that distort and manipulate religious tenets to further their own agendas. These factions, often driven by a mix of political, socio-economic, and personal motives, selectively cherry-pick scriptures, bending them to justify acts of terror and violence under the guise of a 'higher cause'.

The metamorphosis of religion from a source of inner peace to an instrument of external violence is a complex journey. For many adherents of extremist ideologies, the world is seen in stark binaries: believers and non-believers, right and wrong, holy and unholy. Such a black-and-white worldview, while offering clarity, also seeds intolerance, rigidity, and hostility towards any perceived 'other'.

However, it is imperative to differentiate between the religion itself and its extremist outliers. Conflating the two not only does a disservice to countless believers who practice their faith peacefully but also amplifies divisions and misunderstandings. Counteracting religious extremism requires a nuanced understanding of the religion in question, open dialogues with its peaceful leaders, and educational programs that emphasize the nonviolent and inclusive aspects of faith. Only by addressing the root cultural and ideological drivers can societies hope to counter the corrosive effects of religious extremism.

At the heart of ethno-nationalist claims lies a profound sense of identity, belonging, and historical continuity. These sentiments, rooted in shared ethnicity, culture, and history, often drive groups to seek recognition, autonomy, or dominance within a larger nation-state, especially when they perceive themselves as marginalized or oppressed. For many of these groups, their identity is tied to a specific geographic region, often with historical significance. When peaceful negotiations and advocacy fail to secure their objectives, frustration and desperation can ensue. In such contexts, terrorism may emerge as a strategic tool—a means to amplify their grievances, draw international attention, and coerce states into acknowledging their demands.

The logic, from the perspective of these groups, is grounded in the idea of "no voice, no rights." They feel that unless they resort to more drastic measures, their cries for justice, autonomy, or even cultural preservation will continue to be ignored or suppressed. In their view, acts of terror can disrupt the status quo, making the cost of inaction higher for those in power.

However, while the impulse behind such actions might be rooted in genuine grievances, the use of terrorism invariably complicates the path to meaningful dialogue and resolution. It often hardens the stances of both sides and can cause widespread revulsion, especially when innocent civilians are targeted. Addressing ethno-nationalist-driven terrorism requires a delicate balancing act—acknowledging and addressing legitimate grievances while condemning and preventing violent tactics. Only through comprehensive approaches that encompass dialogue, development, and respect for human rights can such challenges be effectively addressed.

In grappling with the specter of terrorism, it becomes clear that the battle is not merely against the act, but the intricate web of socio-economic disparities, political grievances, and deep-seated psychological and cultural factors that underpin it. Understanding terrorism necessitates a panoramic view that acknowledges these myriad drivers and seeks solutions beyond the immediate. The challenge, monumental as it may be, is to address the root causes and not just the manifestations. This entails fostering a world where every group feels heard, valued, and integral to the societal fabric, and where divergent beliefs and experiences converge to create a tapestry rich in diversity yet bound by shared values.

Chapter 4:
Modern Forms of Terrorism

The latter half of the 20th century marked a significant shift in the geopolitical arena, with the end of the colonial era, the Cold War's deep-seated ideological divides, and the onset of globalization. These developments birthed a new breed of terrorism that transcended national boundaries and traditional motives.

As colonial powers retreated, many newly independent nations grappled with internal conflicts, with various ethnic and nationalist groups vying for power or autonomy. The Provisional Irish Republican Army (IRA) in Northern Ireland, the Basque Homeland and Liberty (ETA) in Spain, and the Liberation Tigers of Tamil Eelam (LTTE) in Sri Lanka epitomized this wave of ethno-nationalist terrorism. These groups, driven by a potent mix of ethnic pride, historical grievances, and territorial ambitions, employed violence as a means to achieve political objectives.

The close of the 20th century and the dawn of the 21st century saw the meteoric rise of religious extremist groups. Al-Qaeda's attacks on September 11, 2001, brought this brand of terrorism to the global forefront. Driven by a distorted interpretation of religious texts, groups like Al-Qaeda, Taliban, and ISIS saw themselves as the vanguard of a global religious crusade. Their reach extended far beyond traditional battlefields, with their propaganda inspiring lone-wolf attacks in cities across the West.

The Cold War era saw superpowers engaging in proxy wars, often supporting insurgent groups or rogue regimes to further their geopolitical aims. This state-sponsored terrorism blurred the lines between traditional warfare and terror activities, with states clandestinely furthering their agendas through non-state actors.

The digital age ushered in a new kind of terror. Cyberattacks targeting critical infrastructure, data breaches, and digital propaganda campaigns have become the new norm. State actors, hacktivist groups, and even traditional terror groups recognized the internet's power, not only as a medium for propaganda but also as a tool to wreak havoc, sow discord, or pilfer sensitive information.

The globalization phenomenon, coupled with the internet's omnipresence, has allowed terrorist ideologies to proliferate at an unprecedented rate. Borders have become increasingly porous in the digital age, with radical ideologies just a click away. Moreover, the conflicts in the Middle East, the refugee crises, and the rise of left- and right-wing extremism in the West have added further complexities to the modern terrorism tapestry.

State-sponsored Terrorism

State-sponsored terrorism can be understood as the covert backing or support provided by national governments to terroristic acts and organizations to further their own political, strategic, or ideological aims. This form of terrorism, rather than being the act of an isolated group or individual, bears the weight and backing of a sovereign entity, making it especially potent and, at times, challenging to counteract. Historically, during the era of the Cold War, both superpowers, the United States and the Soviet Union, faced allegations of endorsing such practices. The Soviets were charged with supporting various leftist militant factions, while the U.S. drew criticism for its support of the Contras in Nicaragua, amongst other groups.

The shadow of state-sponsored terrorism has not receded in the modern world. In today's geopolitically charged environment, many nations are suspected of deploying terrorist organizations as instruments of asymmetric warfare. By supporting these groups, nations can undermine and destabilize their regional adversaries without directly committing to a full-fledged, conventional military confrontation. This tactic offers plausible deniability while still inflicting damage upon an opponent, making it an attractive strategy for some nations despite the immense ethical and humanitarian concerns it raises.

Religious Extremism: Jihadism and Beyond

In recent decades, the prominence of jihadist groups such as Al-Qaeda, the Taliban, and ISIS has undoubtedly shaped much of the global discourse on religious extremism and terrorism. These organizations, fueled by a radicalized interpretation of Islam, have orchestrated attacks that have left deep scars in collective memory. Their actions, combined with relentless media coverage, have resulted in a skewed perception, mistakenly equating religious extremism almost exclusively with Islam.

Yet, it is pivotal to understand that extremism is not the sole province of any single faith.

Across the globe, various religions have extremist fringes that distort spiritual teachings to justify violence and exert control. For instance, Myanmar has witnessed violence from radical Buddhist groups against the Rohingya Muslim population. Similarly, in the U.S., extremist Christian factions have, at times, resorted to violence and terroristic tactics in the name of their beliefs. The common thread among all these factions, regardless of religion, is the twisting of spiritual tenets to support an agenda of hate, intolerance, and violence. It is vital for the global community to recognize and address the broader landscape of religious extremism, rather than narrow its focus to any one particular faith.

Ethno-nationalist and Separatist Movements

Ethno-nationalist and separatist movements represent an intricate web of motivations and objectives, deeply rooted in powerful sentiments of identity, historical legacy, and aspirations for self-determination. These movements, as embodied by organizations such as Spain's Basque ETA, the Irish Republican Army (IRA), and the Liberation Tigers of Tamil Eelam (LTTE) in Sri Lanka, are often driven by an unwavering commitment to carve out an independent territory or state that echoes their unique ethnic or nationalistic values and traditions.

At a superficial glance, these movements might seem primarily driven by ethnic or nationalistic sentiments. However, a deeper examination reveals a far more nuanced picture. Their motivations are multi-layered, encompassing not just ethnic pride or historical claims, but also a matrix of intertwined factors that include political ambitions, long-standing historical grievances, perceived or real social injustices, economic disparities, and occasionally, deeply held religious beliefs. These complexities mean that these groups, in their quest for autonomy or independence, are not just fighting for land or territory, but for a space where their cultural, political, and economic aspirations can be fully realized.

The multi-dimensional nature of their struggles is further exacerbated by external challenges. Global geopolitics, regional power dynamics, economic sanctions, and international interventions often shape the trajectories of these movements, sometimes aiding their cause, and at other times, stifling their ambitions. Furthermore, as these movements evolve, they face internal dilemmas, with ideological splits, generational differences, and varying degrees of militancy often coming to the fore.

Understanding these ethno-nationalist and separatist movements requires an approach that goes beyond the conventional. It demands a recognition of the deep-seated complexities that define their objectives, the internal and external challenges they grapple with, and the evolving nature of their struggles. Only through such a comprehensive lens can policymakers, mediators, and stakeholders hope to engage in meaningful dialogues, paving the way for potential resolutions that are equitable, sustainable, and respectful of the diverse aspirations of these groups.

Right-Wing and Left-Wing Extremism

The emergence and growth of extremist ideologies, particularly in the Western sociopolitical environment, have become defining features of the 21st century, and their implications on the fabric of societies are profound. Right-wing extremism, which has seen a notable resurgence in recent years, is anchored in deep-rooted nativist sentiments. This ideology is not just a reflection of political opposition to, say, immigration policies, but a more profound sentiment of cultural and nationalistic preservation. There is an underlying perception among adherents that their cultural or national identity is under siege, primarily due to globalist policies, increasing immigration, and changing societal values. At its most radical, right-wing extremism veers into overt white supremacist and neo-Nazi ideologies, which advocate for racial purity and vehemently oppose multiculturalism.

Contrastingly, left-wing extremism, while distinct in its foundational beliefs and objectives, is equally potent in its challenge to established norms and structures. These groups are motivated by a deep-seated dissatisfaction with capitalist systems, viewing them as inherently exploitative. Their grievances extend to issues like income inequality, corporate malfeasance, and imperialist tendencies of powerful nations. They advocate for a radical restructuring of the economic and political landscape, envisioning a more egalitarian society. Historically, the Red Army Faction in Germany, also known as the Baader-Meinhof Group, serves as an archetype of left-wing extremism. Their campaigns, characterized by kidnappings, bombings, and assassinations, were aimed at destabilizing the state, which they viewed as oppressive and complicit in global imperialism.

Though these extremist wings sit on opposite ends of the political spectrum, they share some similarities. Both are disillusioned with the status quo and believe that the prevailing system — be it cultural, economic, or political — is fundamentally flawed. They are willing to resort to radical means, including violence, to bring about the change they envision. Another shared trait is their propensity to capitalize on societal divisions and discontent, further polarizing communities.

The rise of these extremist ideologies poses a serious challenge to democratic societies. Their growth suggests not just a fringe discontent but potentially deeper, systemic issues that need addressing. For societies to effectively counteract the threats posed by extremism, there needs to be a comprehensive approach. Education plays a crucial role. By promoting critical thinking, tolerance, and open-mindedness from a young age, individuals are better equipped to navigate and challenge extremist views they might encounter later in life. Additionally, ensuring equitable economic opportunities and addressing systemic inequalities can mitigate some of the root causes that feed extremist sentiments.

In the intricate landscape of contemporary terrorism, one thing becomes abundantly clear: it is not a monolithic entity but a mosaic of varied motivations, objectives, and ideologies. The manifestations of terrorism are as diverse as the roots from which they spring, ranging from religious zealotry and ethno-nationalistic sentiments to ideological extremes on both ends of the political spectrum. The diversity of these threats necessitates a profound understanding and appreciation of their distinct nuances. It is not just about countering the acts themselves but addressing the underlying drivers that fuel them.

To create counter-terrorism measures that are genuinely effective, a comprehensive understanding of the threats is essential, moving beyond mere reactive tactics to include proactive prevention. A complete grasp of the multi-layered complexities involved allows for the development of responses that are not just immediate and forceful, but also sustainable and nuanced. This deep understanding will enable policymakers and security experts to anticipate future challenges and mitigate risks before they escalate into crises.

Chapter 5:
Cyber Terrorism and Digital Radicalization - The New Frontiers

In the evolving panorama of global threats, cyber terrorism and digital radicalization have emerged as the new frontiers of concern. Gone are the days when terrorism was exclusively a physical menace; today's adversaries are as skilled in the digital realm as they are on the ground. Cyber terrorism goes beyond mere hacking or data theft; it encompasses sophisticated attacks on critical infrastructures, disruptions of essential services, and even the potential manipulation of public opinion through disinformation campaigns.

Parallelly, the internet has transformed into a fertile ground for radicalization. Online platforms, encrypted messaging apps, and dark web forums serve as virtual echo chambers, where extremist ideologies are propagated, recruits are indoctrinated, and plots are hatched away from prying eyes. This digital shift in terrorism dynamics necessitates a recalibration of counter-terrorism strategies. It underscores the urgency to bolster cyber defenses, enhance digital intelligence capabilities, and foster international cooperation in the virtual realm just as much as in the physical world. The battle against terrorism, once predominantly waged on battlegrounds and streets, now also rages fiercely across servers, networks, screens, and internet cafés.

The Rise of Digital Propaganda

The pervasive reach of the digital realm has dramatically reshaped the contours of radicalization and propaganda dissemination. In this matrix of interconnected devices and platforms, extremist ideologies have found fertile ground, harnessing the capabilities of the online world to embed their narratives into the global consciousness.

Historically, extremist propaganda, especially in video format, was often dismissed due to its subpar production values. However, today's propaganda material, likely shaped by experts well-versed in the art of digital content creation, rivals the quality of mainstream media productions. This level of professionalism makes these videos not just viewable, but engaging, increasing their potential to captivate and indoctrinate audiences. Major social media platforms, originally designed as repositories for user-generated content, inadvertently find themselves in the crosshairs, as they become distribution hubs for this polished extremist content.

Yet, the world of digital propaganda extends beyond high-definition videos and pictures. Encrypted communication tools provide a haven for radicals, allowing them to disseminate their ideologies with a cloak of anonymity and security. By using "end-to-end" encryption, they can communicate, plan, and coordinate without the looming fear of surveillance, complicating efforts to monitor and intercept these channels.

The behemoths of social media, platforms like Twitter and Facebook, despite their commendable intentions to connect the world, have also been ensnared in this web. These platforms have been co-opted into echo chambers, where extremist beliefs not only find voice but are also magnified in the absence of opposing views. Within these closed digital ecosystems, extremist ideologies are not just passively consumed; they are actively reinforced. These platforms inadvertently become accelerators, amplifying radical beliefs, and further entrenching them in the psyche of their users.

Addressing this vast challenge demands an alliance of diverse stakeholders. Tech corporations, entrusted with the stewardship of these platforms, need to continuously enhance their monitoring capabilities, ensuring that extremist content is swiftly detected and removed. Governments, on their part, must balance the delicate act of regulation, ensuring that the free speech spirit of the internet is not stifled while curbing the spread of radical ideologies. Communities, too, play a pivotal role, fostering dialogues that can challenge and deconstruct extremist narratives.

This digital age of extremism underscores a complex conundrum. It is a race against time and technology, where the goal is not merely the removal of content but the creation of a digital space where discourse triumphs over dogma and where ideas are battled with ideas, not with censorship.

Online Radicalization

In the sprawling digital space that has come to dominate our contemporary life, the power of connection and information coexists with the peril of misinformation and radicalization. This online realm, conceived as a testament to human ingenuity and our intrinsic desire to connect across boundaries, has also become a fertile ground for the propagation of extremist ideologies. Platforms such as 4chan, along with specialized subreddits, exemplify the unintended consequences of absolute digital freedom. Originally envisaged as bastions of free thought and dialogue, these platforms have, at times, morphed into echo chambers where unchecked extremist sentiments burgeon, drawing in impressionable minds and fueling divisive ideologies.

Yet, our concerns cannot be limited to these overt platforms alone. The burgeoning world of encrypted messaging, exemplified by platforms like Signal and Telegram, has added another dimension to this challenge. These platforms, while serving as critical tools for ensuring individual privacy in a world rife with surveillance, also double as impenetrable fortresses for those with malicious intent. Shielded by state-of-the-art encryption, extremist groups can strategize, recruit, and propagate their beliefs with relative impunity, far from the scrutinizing glare of intelligence agencies and watchdogs.

Moreover, with the advent of algorithms custom-tailoring content based on user preferences, individuals can unwittingly find themselves trapped in a feedback loop, continuously exposed to extremist views that reinforce and radicalize their existing beliefs. Such algorithms, while designed to enhance user experience, can inadvertently deepen divides and solidify radical beliefs, making deradicalization efforts even more challenging.

Addressing this multi-faceted problem necessitates a comprehensive and multidisciplinary approach. Beyond the immediate need for enhanced cybersecurity protocols and tighter platform regulations, there is a pressing demand for educational initiatives that foster critical thinking and digital literacy. Users equipped with these skills are less susceptible to extremist propaganda. Collaborative efforts between tech giants, governments, and civil society are crucial. Only through a synergy of technology, policy, education, and public awareness can we hope to reclaim the digital realm as a space of genuine connection and enlightenment, steering it away from becoming a hotbed for extremist ideologies.

Cyber Terrorism: Attacks in the Digital Domain

In an age characterized by unprecedented technological advancement, the marriage of terrorism and cyberspace has given rise to a potent and elusive adversary: cyber terrorism. The modern world's pivot towards digitization, while facilitating globalization and innovation, has inadvertently exposed vulnerabilities that can be and have been exploited by those with malicious intent. This form of terrorism is not confined to stereotypical hackers lurking in dimly lit rooms but involves organized extremist networks adeptly leveraging digital platforms to forward their agendas, with a reach extending far beyond simple data breaches.

Visualize, for a moment, the profound implications of a cyber-terrorist attack that incapacitates a country's power supply, disrupts crucial communication channels, or manipulates traffic control systems. Such scenarios, executed from remote locations, could wreak havoc comparable to, if not exceeding, large-scale traditional terror attacks. And in a world where every piece of data is a potential goldmine, cyber terrorists have recognized the immense value of information. By unlawfully obtaining and releasing sensitive data—be it the strategic plans of armed forces, confidential correspondence between government officials, or the personal data of the general populace—they aim to sow discord, tarnish reputations, and erode public trust. This warfare is not just about causing immediate harm; it is a psychological gambit, intended to instill an atmosphere of fear and uncertainty.

Combating the multifarious threats posed by cyber terrorism necessitates a strategy that transcends mere technological defenses. While developing robust cyber-infrastructure, implementing advanced threat detection systems, and adopting cybersecurity research are crucial, there is an overarching need for international solidarity. The borderless nature of the digital realm mandates a collaborative approach. It is imperative for countries to transcend geopolitical rivalries and unite against this common threat, facilitating the exchange of information, pooling technological resources, and jointly developing counter-cyberterrorism protocols.

Furthermore, investing in public education about digital hygiene and awareness can serve as a grassroots countermeasure, fortifying societies from the ground up. As the digital tapestry of our world continues to expand and intricately weave itself into the fabric of our daily lives, the onus is on governments, tech industries, and global communities to ensure that this realm remains a beacon of progress, not a conduit for chaos.

Countermeasures and Challenges

Addressing this dark underbelly of cyberspace, governments worldwide, in synergy with prominent tech entities, are relentlessly striving to implement comprehensive surveillance and monitoring mechanisms. By scouring online spaces, these collaborations aim to detect, identify, and subsequently mitigate the spread of extremist content, fostering an online environment that echoes the values of peace, unity, and understanding.

Recognizing that technological solutions can only go so far; the global community is increasingly emphasizing the pivotal role of digital literacy and education. This approach is anchored in the belief that a well-informed and critically thinking populace can act as an intrinsic firewall against the dangers of digital radicalization. By nurturing the youth—often the most susceptible demographic—with skills to discern the authenticity and intent of online content, we not only protect them but also enable them to be vigilant custodians of the digital realm.

However, as these countermeasures evolve and become more sophisticated, they inadvertently usher in a host of ethical dilemmas. The aggressive surveillance mechanisms, though noble in intent, inadvertently threaten the cherished principles of individual privacy. Thus, society grapples with a profound ethical dilemma: how to ensure the digital world remains a sanctuary free from radical ideologies, while simultaneously safeguarding the fundamental rights and freedoms that individuals hold dear in this space. As the world moves further into the digital age, forging a path that harmoniously reconciles safety with personal freedoms will demand collaborative, transparent, and adaptive strategies, lest we compromise the very ideals we seek to uphold.

Case Study

Islamic State of Iraq and Syria: The rise of ISIS, or the Islamic State of Iraq and Syria, in the early 2010s sent shockwaves throughout the world, not just for its brutal ground tactics, but also its unprecedented use of the digital space for propaganda and recruitment. Labelled by many as the 'Digital Caliphate', ISIS masterfully harnessed the power of the internet to advance its radical ideologies. Their digital strategy was sophisticated, multi-faceted, and surprisingly modern. They produced slick propaganda videos with high production values, comparable to professional films, which showcased both their military might and their vision of a utopian Islamic state. This cinematic approach was designed to captivate, indoctrinate, and eventually draw sympathizers from across the globe.

Parallel to their visual campaign, ISIS demonstrated a keen understanding of the influence of social media platforms. Twitter, in particular, became a crucial tool for their operations. With thousands of accounts, they disseminated their messages, shared graphic content to instill fear, and actively recruited vulnerable individuals from diverse corners of the world. The immediacy and widespread reach of the platform made it an ideal medium for their objectives, enabling real-time communication and the propagation of their extremist narrative.

However, as with all things in the digital realm, the visibility and traceability of their actions eventually became their Achilles heel. Global tech companies, governments, and independent cyber activists began concerted efforts to counteract the group's online influence. Massive takedowns of accounts, digital forensics to trace the originators of extremist content, and collaborative efforts to create counter-narratives gradually chipped away at ISIS's digital dominance. The eventual decline of their 'Digital Caliphate' offers a potent case study into the intricacies of warfare in the age of the internet. It underscores the reality that while digital space can amplify extremist voices, it also provides the tools and collaborative possibilities to challenge, combat, and eventually dismantle such threats.

Separately, the hidden depths of the internet, often referred to as the darknet, exists in stark contrast to the surface web we navigate daily. Encrypted and intentionally hidden, this subterranean digital realm is a haven for illicit activities ranging from the sale of narcotics and arms to the ominous exchanges concerning potential terrorist plots. Its structure, decentralized and difficult to access without specialized software, offers layers of anonymity and security to its users, making it an alluring platform for those with nefarious intentions.

Counter-terrorism agencies, well aware of the threats posed by this digital labyrinth, face the arduous task of penetrating its depths. The challenges are manifold. While the open internet is relatively transparent, allowing for easier monitoring and intervention, the darknet is designed to obfuscate and protect user identities and activities. Thus, traditional surveillance methods often fall short. Instead, a combination of advanced digital forensics, undercover operations, and collaboration with cybersecurity experts is essential to pierce through the veil of the darknet.

Furthermore, as we dive deeper into the digital age, the broader virtual realm beyond just the darknet is becoming a focal point in the fight against terrorism. With the acceleration of technological advancements, extremist factions continue to adapt, exploiting new tools and platforms to further their agendas. This constant evolution underscores the necessity for counter-terrorism efforts to be equally dynamic, embracing cutting-edge technologies and strategies to stay a step ahead. The digital world, with its promise of connection and knowledge-sharing, paradoxically also emerges as a frontier of potential threats. Understanding its intricacies, especially the shadowed corridors of the darknet, is no longer just a task for tech enthusiasts but a paramount mission for those dedicated to global security and peace.

Chapter 6:
Lone Wolf Terrorism - The Rise of the Individual Attacker

The emergence of lone wolf attackers, in the ever-evolving landscape of terrorism, has added a complex layer of unpredictability and challenges. Historically, counter-terrorism strategies have been centered around dismantling organized extremist groups, relying on intelligence to predict and preempt large-scale attacks. However, the lone wolf phenomenon — characterized by individuals who act without direct command or overt connection to a larger group — disrupts this conventional model. These individuals often operate under the radar, their motivations a blend of personal grievances, ideological radicalization, and sometimes psychological issues. Their isolated nature makes them harder to detect; they leave behind fewer communication trails and are less likely to raise red flags than a coordinated group might.

Furthermore, their actions can be impulsive, spurred by an online article, a personal experience, or an immediate sense of injustice, making their attacks harder to anticipate. The digital age, with its vast online echo chambers, plays a role in the rise of this phenomenon, offering platforms for radicalization, while also affording anonymity. Confronting the challenge of lone wolf terrorism demands a reimagining of conventional counter-terrorism measures. It requires a deeper societal involvement, heightened public vigilance, and innovative intelligence approaches that can parse through vast amounts of online data to detect early signs of radicalization among seemingly ordinary individuals.

Understanding the Lone Wolf

The lone wolf terrorist presents an enigma that sharply contrasts with the more traditional, structured terrorist networks that have historically been the focus of security agencies. Rooted in their autonomy, these individuals, operating on the fringes of society, embody an unpredictable and evolving threat.

One of the primary characteristics of lone wolf terrorists is their distinct independence from structured terrorist organizations. Unlike their counterparts who might be embedded within larger, hierarchical organizations, lone wolves act outside these frameworks, often without receiving direct training, resources, or specific directives. This separation from a guiding hand means that their motivations, while possibly inspired by broader extremist ideologies, are usually deeply personal. Such motivations could range from individual grievances, societal disillusionment, or perceived slights that push them towards radical actions.

Their operational methods are varied and often reflect a fusion of their personal skills, local knowledge, and available resources. For instance, while one lone wolf might employ sophisticated cyber tactics, another might resort to simple, yet brutal physical violence. This lack of a consistent modus operandi, devoid of recognizable patterns often associated with larger terrorist groups, poses a significant challenge for prevention and early detection.

Moreover, the absence of discernible communication or recruitment channels adds another layer of complexity to tracking their activities. Since they operate largely in isolation, they leave behind a much-reduced digital or logistical footprint. They may not attend known radicalizing locations, participate in conspicuous online forums, or engage in overt financial transactions tied to extremist activities.

Despite their potentially reduced scale of operations, the impact of lone wolf attacks on society can be disproportionately profound. The sheer unpredictability of these individuals, combined with their ability to blend seamlessly into their communities, creates a pervasive sense of unease. Citizens begin to grapple with the unsettling notion that anyone, be it a neighbor, coworker, or a casual acquaintance, could harbor extremist sentiments and act upon them. This challenges established counter-terrorism strategies, necessitating new approaches that account for the nuanced, multi-layered nature of this threat. It is not just about tracking networks but understanding individual trajectories of radicalization and finding ways to intervene before they culminate in acts of terror.

The motivations that propel lone wolves towards acts of terror can be both diverse and deeply personal, differing significantly from the collective objectives of organized extremist groups. At the heart of their radical journey often lies a mosaic of personal grievances. These can stem from personal failures, perceived societal slights, or instances of discrimination and ostracization. Such feelings of disillusionment or resentment might make them susceptible to the allure of extremist ideologies, which promise validation, retribution, or a higher purpose.

The digital age, particularly the vast expanses of the internet, has transformed the radicalization landscape. Online platforms, encrypted messaging services, and shadowy forums serve as echo chambers where extremist ideologies are magnified and unchallenged. For the solitary individual grappling with feelings of resentment or isolation, the internet offers a treasure trove of extremist content—videos, manifestos, and chat forums—that can validate and intensify their radical beliefs. These platforms not only disseminate extremist propaganda but also offer a semblance of community and belonging, further solidifying their extremist leanings.

Moreover, the instantaneous nature of digital communication means that events from distant parts of the world can be relayed in near real-time, amplifying personal grievances with global injustices. For instance, a lone wolf in one country might be spurred into action by perceived injustices or attacks on their ideological or ethnic kin thousands of miles away, thanks to the immediate access of online media.

While the internet is a significant factor, it is essential to recognize that lone wolf radicalization is not solely a digital phenomenon. Personal experiences, interactions, and local socio-political environments intertwine with digital influences, creating a potent cocktail of radicalization factors. Decoding this intricate web is crucial for preemptive intervention, ensuring that feelings of alienation or revenge do not find an outlet in acts of terror.

The Challenges in Detection

Addressing the menace of lone wolf terrorism introduces unique hurdles for intelligence and law enforcement agencies. Historically, intelligence operations have often hinged on the ability to monitor and intercept communications within and between extremist networks. By tapping into these channels, agencies could glean insights into potential plots, strategies, and hierarchical structures, thereby preemptively thwarting terrorist acts. However, when confronted with the lone wolf paradigm, this conventional playbook becomes mute.

The inherent solitary nature of lone wolf actors means there is a stark absence of the usual communication "chatter" that agencies are trained to detect. These individuals do not necessarily rely on extensive planning sessions, collaborations, or leadership approvals that organized groups might. Their operations are often impromptu, driven by personal motivations and immediate triggers, which makes their actions less predictable. Moreover, if they do communicate or seek inspiration, it might be through encrypted platforms, private forums, or even seemingly benign mainstream platforms, making detection even more challenging.

Furthermore, lone wolves, due to their detachment from established extremist organizations, may not fit the traditional terrorist profile, further complicating surveillance and profiling efforts. They could be embedded in everyday life, holding regular jobs, and maintaining typical routines until they decide to act on their radicalized beliefs. This chameleon-like ability to blend into society, combined with the absence of typical communication markers, requires a paradigm shift in counter-terrorism approaches, emphasizing community engagement, behavioral analysis, and digital forensics.

The strategy and intent behind terrorist attacks orchestrated by organized extremist groups are often tethered to larger ideological or political objectives. These groups tend to target sites of symbolic significance, high-profile landmarks, or locations that would elicit maximum global attention and media coverage, thereby amplifying their message. This makes the task of predicting and fortifying potential targets somewhat more conceivable. However, the realm of lone wolf terrorism operates on a different axis of unpredictability.

Lone wolves, unburdened by organizational hierarchies or the need for collective consensus, often operate on deeply personal motivations, grievances, or impulses. As such, their choice of target can diverge from the conventional "high-value" sites. Instead, they might strike soft targets – local gathering spots, community events, small businesses, or even seemingly random public spaces. These are places where people ordinarily feel safe and are less guarded, making them especially vulnerable. The inherent randomness of such attacks not only magnifies public fear but also stretches the resources of security agencies.

This shift towards targeting soft and unpredictable targets is not merely tactical but also psychological. By focusing on everyday locations, lone wolves amplify the undercurrent of fear among the masses. No longer are only the iconic landmarks at risk, but every ordinary locale becomes a potential ground zero. This change poses a daunting challenge to security agencies. Pre-empting an organized terrorist attack is challenging in itself; however, with lone wolves, the challenge is magnified exponentially. It becomes a game of vast probabilities with a sprawling landscape of potential targets, limited actionable intelligence, and the daunting realization that every place is vulnerable. This unpredictability necessitates not only an agile and expansive security infrastructure but also an in-depth societal engagement to detect signs of radicalization early on and thwart potential threats.

Historically, the path to radicalization was considered a protracted one, often influenced by a combination of personal experiences, long-term affiliations with extremist groups, and a steady consumption of radical ideologies over time. However, the current landscape has witnessed a worrying trend: the acceleration of this radicalization process. Some individuals now become radicalized in mere months, or in extreme cases, even weeks. The factors fueling this accelerated timeline are multifaceted and interconnected.

The digital revolution has significantly transformed the way extremist ideologies are propagated and consumed. The internet offers a vast ocean of information, and with it, an unfettered access to extremist content that was once difficult to obtain. Social media platforms, for instance, are not just tools for communication but have inadvertently become potent echo chambers where extremist beliefs are amplified and reaffirmed. Encrypted messaging apps, while providing privacy to its users, also offer safe havens for radical ideologues to spread their message without fear of detection. Then there is the dark web, a more covert space, where extremist forums thrive, often beyond the reach of traditional surveillance.

The barrage of real-time news and the ability to instantly witness global events, often with distressing imagery and narratives, further stoke the fires of alienation and anger. For a vulnerable individual, the relentless exposure to perceived injustices can create an overwhelming sense of urgency, pushing them swiftly towards extremist ideologies as they seek answers or avenues for action.

Adding complexity to this is the personalized nature of online content. Algorithms designed to feed users content based on their preferences can inadvertently narrow their worldview, reinforcing their beliefs and pushing them further down the rabbit hole of extremism.
Then there are personal catalysts. An individual experiencing personal traumas, grievances, or a profound sense of injustice can find solace in extremist narratives that resonate with their experiences. The online extremist communities can offer them not only ideological validation but also a sense of belonging.

This rapid radicalization poses a monumental challenge for security agencies and counter-terrorism experts. The window to detect, monitor, and act on these rapidly radicalizing threats is dramatically reduced. The traditional markers or indicators of radicalization might be less evident or entirely absent. As such, it necessitates the development of more nuanced, agile, and technologically advanced strategies that can keep pace with this evolving threat, detect early signs of rapid radical intent, and deploy swift intervention mechanisms to thwart any impending acts of violence.

Case Studies

2011 Massacre in Utøya, Norway: In July 2011, the world was shaken by the chilling actions of Anders Behring Breivik in Norway. The meticulousness with which he executed his two-phase attack was a grim testament to the dangers posed by lone wolf terrorists. Beginning with a powerful car bomb detonated in Oslo's government quarter, Breivik inflicted immediate devastation. However, the horror was compounded mere hours later when, disguised as a police officer, he embarked on a merciless shooting spree at a youth camp on the island of Utøya. The aftermath was harrowing: 77 lives taken, and a nation traumatized.

What perplexed many was the seemingly sudden eruption of such virulent violence from an individual who lacked direct affiliations with known extremist organizations. The answers were buried in his 1,500-page manifesto, where Breivik described his warped worldview. Within its pages, he professed an alarming disdain for multiculturalism, left-wing ideologies, and what he perceived as the "Islamization" of Europe. Breivik postulated himself as a modern-day crusader, waging war against these forces.

This manifesto also highlighted the role of the internet in shaping his ideologies. Breivik had been marinating in a digital environment of far-right forums, conspiracy websites, and anti-Islam content. The echo chambers he frequented only amplified his beliefs, pushing him further into radicalization.

Breivik's case underscores the multifaceted nature of lone wolf terrorism. While his motivations were rooted in political and cultural grievances, the methods of radicalization, planning, and execution were undeniably contemporary, benefiting from the vast reservoir of information and ideological reinforcement available online. His actions serve as a stark reminder that even in seemingly peaceful societies, the seeds of extremism can find fertile ground in the minds of individuals who feel alienated, threatened, or ideologically oppressed. The challenge remains not just in countering organized terror outfits but also in recognizing and mitigating the factors that can push solitary individuals toward committing acts of unparalleled violence.

2016 Pulse Nightclub Shooting, Florida: In 2016, a grim episode unfolded in Orlando, Florida, when Omar Mateen launched an assault on the Pulse nightclub, resulting in the tragic loss of 49 innocent lives and scores more injured. The attack was not only one of the deadliest mass shootings in U.S. history but also a somber example of the unpredictable nature of lone wolf terrorism.

Mateen's motivations for carrying out the assault were intricate, a blend of personal animosities and broader ideological leanings. Reports surfaced after the attack suggesting that he may have frequented the nightclub before and struggled with his own sexuality, raising questions about the extent to which personal factors played into his decision to target Pulse specifically.

On the ideological front, while Mateen reportedly declared allegiance to ISIS during the attack, his understanding of Islamist extremist groups seemed muddled. He had previously expressed sympathies for different radical factions, some of which were even at odds with ISIS. This points to the influence of online radicalization, where an overwhelming influx of extremist content can sometimes lead to a mishmash of radical beliefs in individuals.

The Orlando attack underscored the challenge in categorizing and understanding the motivations of lone wolf attackers. While Mateen's actions were certainly influenced by radical ideologies he encountered online, personal grievances and inner conflicts played an equally crucial role. The tragedy emphasized the pressing need for both online monitoring of extremist content and better community-based interventions. It also demonstrated the dangers of an environment where personal struggles collide with readily available extremist narratives, producing deadly outcomes. The case of Omar Mateen serves as a stark reminder that the roots of radicalization can be multifarious and intertwined.

2017 Las Vegas Shooting: On the night of October 1, 2017, Las Vegas, typically a city of glitz and entertainment, became the epicenter of a tragic "lone wolf" attack—marking it as the deadliest mass shooting in modern U.S. history. The bustling Route 91 Harvest music festival, drawing a crowd of around 22,000 attendees, was violently interrupted when Stephen Paddock, a 64-year-old retiree perched on the 32nd floor of the Mandalay Bay Resort and Casino, unleashed a torrent of bullets. Preparing for this attack, Paddock, in a chilling display of foresight, had amassed an arsenal of 23 firearms in his hotel room. He had also modified these weapons transforming semi-automatic firearms into near-automatic weapons.

As country artist Jason Aldean played to the unsuspecting crowd below, the festival grounds became a scene of unparalleled horror, with bullets raining down for an agonizing ten minutes. The aftermath was devastating: 58 individuals lost their lives and over 500 others were wounded.

The swift response of law enforcement and emergency services was commendable, as they rushed to Mandalay Bay while grappling with the sheer scale of the calamity. The vicinity of the world-famous Las Vegas Strip was swiftly locked down, and other nearby hotels initiated evacuations or increased security measures.

Further investigation painted a chilling picture of Paddock's meticulous planning: surveillance cameras set up for monitoring, a strategically chosen hotel room, and an overwhelming stockpile of ammunition. Yet, even with these details, Paddock's reasoning remains shrouded in mystery. In-depth inquiries could not trace any links to global terrorist organizations or any discernible personal motives.

2023 Covenant School Shooting, Nashville: The quiet morning of March 27, 2023, in Nashville, Tennessee, was shattered by an act of lone wolf terrorism. The Covenant School found itself in the crosshairs of a former student, Aiden Hale. A transgender man, Hale's lone wolf attack ended with six innocent lives lost, among them, three nine-year-old children.

A few minutes after Hale made his foreboding entry. An eerie Instagram message was sent suggesting a dark intent. This "suicide note" spurred one of Hale's friends into desperately reaching out for help. But the lone wolf's actions swiftly unfolded. By 10:11 a.m., Hale gained entry into the school, by firing through a set of glass doors.

The Metropolitan Nashville Police Department (MNPD), alerted by an initial call at 10:13 a.m., walked into a scene straight out of a nightmare. With more than 150 rounds fired, the aftermath revealed the heart-wrenching toll: six lives taken too soon. The siege came to an end when responding offices shot Hale dead.

Digging into the background of this lone wolf, Aiden Hale, formerly known as Audrey Elizabeth Hale, had personal ties to the school, amplifying the shock of the community. Beyond personal aspects, Hale had a promising career as an illustrator and graphic designer. But amidst the vestiges of his life, the motives for his extreme actions remained elusive. Although investigators discovered maps and an apparent manifesto, these items were, at best, ambiguous, with descriptions ranging from "rambling" to inconclusive.

In the aftermath of the lone wolf's assault, a grieving community rallied together. The Covenant School sought both privacy and healing. The Covenant School's lone wolf attack not only propelled a narrative of grief but also invoked intense dialogues around safety, identity, and the challenges of confronting singular acts of terror in today's world. This tragedy underscores the complexities and unpredictability of modern society, pushing for greater vigilance and unity.

2023 The Fargo Ambush: On July 14, 2023, in Fargo, North Dakota, an ambush targeting police unfolded that highlighted the challenges of preempting Lone Wolf attacks. Mohamad Barakat, a Syrian national, targeted officers at the scene of a minor traffic accident. The quick response by Officer Robinson, who killed Barakat, likely prevented a larger tragedy, but the event left one officer dead and two others wounded, along with a bystander. The subsequent investigation revealed Barakat's alarming internet searches related to mass violence and uncovered an arsenal inside his car, including firearms, thousands of rounds of ammunition, a homemade grenade, and other explosive materials. This evidence suggests that Barakat had intended to target a larger public event, possibly the Downtown Fargo Street Fair, raising questions about the effectiveness of current online monitoring systems in identifying such threats.

The incident raises multiple questions regarding security and law enforcement preparedness. For instance, the weaponry in Barakat's car indicated planning for a larger attack, pointing to gaps in online monitoring systems that failed to flag his alarming internet behavior. Barakat's lone-wolf profile—acting without apparent affiliation to terror groups or obvious hatred towards the police—adds another layer of complexity. Existing countermeasures include enhanced internet monitoring, public awareness campaigns for reporting suspicious behavior, and specialized officer training for 'active shooter' scenarios. However, these measures often grapple with ethical concerns like potential infringement on personal privacy and the risk of profiling or stigmatizing certain communities.

Ultimately, the Fargo case serves as a somber lesson in the unpredictability of terrorist threats and the urgency of developing nuanced, ethical, and effective countermeasures. The swift action of Officer Robinson possibly averted a more catastrophic event, yet the ambush itself remains a wake-up call for revising and improving current strategies in identifying and neutralizing potential threats. It underlines the need for multi-dimensional approaches that not only adapt to evolving risks but also address the ethical complexities inherent in counter-terrorism efforts.

Countermeasures and Solutions

With the internet's pervasive reach, and the anonymity it offers, extremist ideologies have found a space where they can flourish unchecked and radicalize vulnerable individuals at an unprecedented scale. Recognizing the escalating threat posed by this online radicalization, particularly in the context of lone wolf terrorists, governments and intelligence agencies worldwide have embarked on a mission to reclaim and monitor these virtual spaces, with enhanced surveillance being a cornerstone of their strategy.

Enhanced surveillance is not merely about keeping tabs on potential threats; it is about weaving a protective net over the vast expanses of the digital realm. This involves a multifaceted approach. Governments are harnessing the power of artificial intelligence to sift through massive amounts of data, identifying patterns that might allude to extremist leanings. Machine learning algorithms are trained to detect and flag extremist rhetoric, while sophisticated cyber tools track the movement and sharing of radical content across platforms, from mainstream social media to encrypted messaging apps and the elusive corridors of the dark web.

But the challenges are manifold. The sheer volume of online interactions and the global nature of the internet mean that potential threats can emerge from any corner of the world. Moreover, as surveillance tools evolve, so do the methods employed by those intent on spreading hate. Encryption, VPNs, and decentralized platforms pose significant hurdles in the path of surveillance.

While the technical challenges are considerable, the ethical dilemmas posed by enhanced surveillance are even more intricate. At what point does surveillance become an intrusion? How do governments ensure that the right to privacy, a cornerstone of democratic societies, is not compromised? These questions underscore the delicate balancing act involved in ensuring security while upholding civil liberties.

However, amidst the challenges and critiques, the importance of enhanced surveillance in the contemporary counter-terrorism toolkit remains undeniable. In a world where a single online post can inspire devastating acts of violence, the imperative to monitor, understand, and act upon the digital markers of radicalization is both urgent and critical. As the lines between the virtual and real worlds continue to blur, ensuring the safety and security of societies requires a vigilant watch over both domains, ensuring that the echo chambers of online extremism are identified and neutralized.

At the heart of effective counter-terrorism lies not just the machinery of surveillance and law enforcement but the vibrant, often untapped reservoir of community insight and vigilance. As the threat of lone wolf terrorism progresses, the importance of building and maintaining robust ties with communities becomes paramount. Community outreach, in this context, is not merely a strategy; it is a fundamental shift towards a more collaborative, grassroots approach to national security.

Communities, especially those tightly knit and closely aligned with specific cultural or religious identities, often possess an intimate knowledge of their members. They are the first to notice subtle behavioral changes, shifts in beliefs, or the embrace of extremist ideologies among their peers. By fostering trust and open lines of communication with these communities, authorities can tap into this localized knowledge, gaining early warnings about individuals who might be on the path to radicalization.

But the benefits of community outreach extend beyond intelligence gathering. It offers a platform for dialogue, dispelling misconceptions, addressing grievances, and promoting mutual understanding. When communities feel heard, valued, and engaged, they are more likely to become proactive partners in counter-terrorism efforts. Furthermore, outreach initiatives can also encompass educational programs, targeting especially the youth, to build resilience against extremist propaganda and offer counter-narratives that champion peace, unity, and coexistence.

Yet, for community outreach to truly be successful, it must be genuine and reciprocal. It is not just about extracting information but about building relationships, understanding concerns, and jointly crafting solutions. In an age where the tendrils of radicalization can silently seep into homes through digital channels, the protective shield of a vigilant, informed, and empowered community becomes an invaluable asset in the fight against terrorism. By placing communities at the forefront of counter-terrorism, authorities not only gain allies but also reinforce the very fabric of society, making it more resistant to the divisive forces of extremism.

In the intricate web of factors driving lone wolf terrorism, mental health stands out as both a salient and often overlooked dimension. Numerous lone wolf attackers, past and present, exhibit an array of psychological distress, unaddressed trauma, or undiagnosed mental health disorders. While it is crucial not to oversimplify or stigmatize mental health challenges by directly equating them with propensities for violent extremism, the correlation is undeniable. Recognizing this interplay, a holistic approach to counter-terrorism necessarily incorporates robust mental health initiatives.

Addressing mental health is not just about therapeutic interventions for those already diagnosed. It is about fostering an environment where mental well-being is prioritized, stigma is dismantled, and seeking help is normalized. Early detection of mental health issues can lead to timely interventions, potentially diverting individuals from the paths of radicalization that may exploit their vulnerabilities. Moreover, community mental health programs can act as buffers, providing support networks and tools for resilience.

Furthermore, in a digital age where online radicalization is rampant, the isolation or desolation felt by individuals with mental health challenges can be exacerbated by extremist narratives they encounter online. Comprehensive mental health care, in this context, serves a dual purpose: healing the individual and safeguarding society. By investing in mental health awareness, care, and infrastructure, societies are not only enhancing the well-being of their citizens but are also erecting a crucial line of defense against the allure of extremist ideologies that might prey on the psychologically vulnerable.

The lone wolf phenomenon underscores the evolving nature of terrorism in the 21st century and is a stark reminder that in the ever-changing theater of terrorism, responses must be as adaptive, many-sided, and forward-thinking as the threats they seek to counteract. Understanding and addressing this challenge requires a blend of technology, community engagement, and a deep understanding of the individual psyche.

Chapter 7:
The Concept of Blood Debt in Extremist Interpretations of Islam

The term "blood debt" has emerged as a highly controversial and often misinterpreted concept within radical strands of Islamic thought. Serving both as a basis for legitimizing violent acts and as a recruiting mechanism for extremist groups, the idea has far-reaching consequences. Its potency lies not only in its call for retribution but also in its capacity to attract individuals to extremist causes, further complicating efforts to combat terrorism.

It is of paramount importance to separate the extremist use of "blood debt" from the broader, more nuanced theological perspectives within mainstream Islam. While Islam encompasses a diverse array of teachings and schools of thought, the extremist version of blood debt represents a selective, often distorted, interpretation of the religion. This divergence underscores the risks of conflating extremist ideologies with the faith as a whole.

This comprehensive discussion aims to navigate the intricate labyrinth of how "blood debt" is conceptualized and mobilized by extremist factions. By looking into its historical roots, examining the theological frameworks that extremists use to justify it, and assessing its role in contemporary acts of terror, we hope to offer a well-rounded understanding of the concept.

Analyzing the extremist concept of "blood debt" is not merely an intellectual exercise. Its impact reverberates across global security landscapes, making it an urgent topic for scholars, policymakers, and the general public alike. As a pivotal factor in radicalization processes, the term is more than just an abstract notion; it is a real and immediate catalyst for actions that result in loss of life and social discord.

Mainstream Islamic Jurisprudence

In the realm of conventional Islamic law, the term that most closely resembles the idea of a "blood debt" is "Diyah," which is often translated as "blood money." The practice is governed by a complex set of ethical and legal stipulations. According to this traditional understanding, if someone is killed—whether intentionally or unintentionally—the victim's family has the right to demand financial compensation from the person responsible. This compensation is intended to serve as a form of reparation for the loss, and if both parties agree to this arrangement, the case can be settled without further legal action.

Contrastingly, extremist factions within Islam manipulate the concept of Diyah, twisting its original intent and ethical framework. These groups co-opt the term to justify acts of violence and terrorism, far exceeding the ethical and legal constraints traditionally associated with it. Their interpretation serves not just as a theological justification for violence but also as a recruitment tool to draw individuals into their extremist ideologies.

While the term "Diyah" exists within mainstream Islamic jurisprudence as a regulated, ethical practice, its extremist interpretations diverge significantly from its original context. These distortions serve as a basis for justifying heinous acts that are not endorsed by mainstream Islamic teachings.

Extremist Interpretations: A Warped Perspective

Within certain extremist factions embedded in the Islamic faith, the concept of blood debt is frequently manipulated to provide an appearance of religious legitimacy for violent acts, including terrorism. According to their skewed interpretation, the death of Muslims at the hands of those labeled as "infidels"—whether it be in war zones or as a result of policies perceived to be against Islamic principles—creates a so-called blood debt. This debt, they argue, can only be "repaid" or "settled" through corresponding acts of violence against those they deem responsible or even vaguely associated.

This twisted version of blood debt serves as a theological cloak under which extremists can execute attacks that make no distinction between military and civilian targets. Such interpretations are not only a misuse of the concept but are also in direct violation of mainstream Islamic jurisprudence, which has precise regulations governing warfare, violence, and the sanctity of human life.

These extremist viewpoints do not exist in a vacuum; they contribute to perpetual cycles of violence and retribution. By employing this adulterated form of the blood debt principle as a rallying cry, extremist groups can mobilize their followers into actions that heighten existing conflicts, exacerbate social and religious tensions, and deepen divisions among communities. These actions, often marked by brutality, add fuel to an already volatile situation, setting the stage for an ongoing cycle of violence that seems to have no end.

The misuse of the concept of blood debt by extremist factions within Islam serves as a poignant example of how religious principles can be distorted to serve violent ends. It not only violates the foundational tenets of Islamic law and ethics but also contributes to a vicious cycle of violence, undermining peace efforts and causing untold suffering. Understanding this misuse is crucial for both combating extremism and fostering dialogue that can lead to genuine peace and reconciliation.

Ideological Convergence: Blood Debt and the Call to Jihad

In the ideological universe of extremist factions within Islam, the notion of blood debt frequently intersects with calls for Jihad, commonly understood as a "holy war" within these extremist contexts. For these groups, the perception that Muslims worldwide are under siege becomes an integral part of their overarching narrative, which posits a never-ending struggle between Islam and perceived enemies, often identified as the West or other so-called "Enemies of Islam."

Utilizing the concept of blood debt, extremist ideologues aim to galvanize their followers into joining what they portray as a defensive holy war. This skewed concept of a blood debt serves a dual purpose; not only does it provide a theological justification for acts of violence, but it also acts as an effective recruitment tool. The idea that there exists a "debt" that needs to be "repaid" taps into notions of honor, duty, and justice that resonate powerfully with potential recruits.

This union of blood debt and Jihad creates a self-reinforcing cycle: the concept of blood debt justifies violence and lures new members, while the influx of new members perpetuates the notion of an ongoing Jihad. This cycle serves to continuously feed into the extremist narrative, providing both manpower and ideological fuel for the continuation of violence and recruitment activities.

Understanding this ideological convergence is crucial for dismantling the infrastructures of radicalization and developing strategies to counter extremist interpretations effectively. It shows how extremist groups manipulate religious and cultural concepts to advance their agendas, deepening cycles of conflict and retribution.

Case Studies

Al-Qaeda and the 9/11 Attacks: Al-Qaeda, under the leadership of Osama bin Laden, was the mastermind behind the devastating attacks on September 11, 2001, targeting significant landmarks in the United States. In the weeks and months following the event, the organization released a series of manifestos, interviews, and propaganda videos. Central to their justification for the attacks was the concept of "blood debt." According to Al-Qaeda's extremist interpretation of this notion, the U.S., by maintaining military bases in Saudi Arabia (considered holy land) and by involving itself in conflicts that resulted in Muslim casualties, had accumulated a "blood debt" that required repayment.

By employing the concept of "blood debt," Al-Qaeda attempted to provide a theological veneer to their acts of terror. They argued that because the United States and its allies had allegedly been responsible for Muslim deaths through military actions and sanctions, especially in countries like Iraq and Afghanistan, a blood debt had been established. They asserted that this debt could only be settled through reciprocal violence aimed at Americans.

One of the most insidious aspects of invoking "blood debt" was its efficacy as a recruitment tool. Al-Qaeda used this twisted logic to motivate and radicalize individuals who were already inclined to hold hostile views toward the United States. By framing their actions as a form of "justice," the organization attracted new members, thereby regenerating its manpower and sustaining its operations.

ISIS and the Yazidi Genocide: ISIS engaged in a campaign of unimaginable cruelty against the Yazidi community in Northern Iraq, particularly around the Sinjar region. Starting in 2014, the extremist group began a series of targeted killings, enslavements, and sexual abuses. The Yazidi community, already marginalized and stigmatized for their unique religious beliefs, found themselves at the center of a horrific genocidal campaign.

ISIS employed a twisted interpretation of the concept of "blood debt" to justify their inhuman acts. The group labeled the Yazidis as "devil-worshippers," a gross misrepresentation of the Yazidi faith, to argue that they deserved extermination or enslavement. In their extremist ideology, the Yazidis had accumulated a so-called "blood debt" that needed to be repaid through extreme violence. This interpretation went as far as to claim that the Yazidis owed a historical "debt" to "true believers," although this claim had no basis in mainstream Islamic teachings or history.

The propaganda machine of ISIS went into overdrive to spread this distorted rationale. Using social media platforms, pamphlets, and videos, they presented their actions against the Yazidis as repayment for this imagined "blood debt." This propaganda was designed not only to dehumanize the Yazidis but also to serve as a powerful recruiting tool. Individuals already radicalized or those who were susceptible to such radicalization found a twisted sense of purpose and community in these messages. This further perpetuated the cycle of violence and recruited more individuals to partake in the atrocities.

The Yazidi community still grapples with the trauma of this genocidal campaign, with many survivors suffering from lifelong psychological and physical scars. Moreover, the use of the "blood debt" concept in this context had broader implications for the international community. It highlighted the depths to which extremist ideologies could sink to justify acts of terror and genocide.

The Taliban and the Afghan Government: The Taliban made a dramatic return to power in Afghanistan in 2021. After being ousted by a U.S.-led coalition in 2001, they found sanctuary in neighboring Pakistan, where they regrouped and strategized for their resurgence. Within less than a decade from their initial defeat, they began to reclaim territory, culminating in their full return to power by August 2021. This effectively dismantled the Afghan government, which had been supported by the United States and its allies for nearly two decades.

Central to the Taliban's resurgence and sustained violence is their manipulation of the Islamic concept of "blood debt." They argued that the Afghan government, which was backed by Western nations, was guilty of Muslim deaths, thereby accruing a "blood debt" that must be settled. This interpretation, far removed from mainstream Islamic teachings, served to justify their campaign of violence and terrorism.

Exploiting their extensive network of madrasas (Islamic religious schools), as well as modern propaganda tools like social media, the Taliban disseminated its extremist interpretation of "blood debt" to indoctrinate new generations of fighters. These madrasas served as ideological breeding grounds where young minds were molded to view the world through the lens of extremist thought, becoming the fighters of tomorrow committed to "settling" this supposed debt. The invocation of "blood debt" served multiple purposes for the Taliban. It not only provided a theological rationale for their acts of violence but also acted as a potent recruitment tool.

Each of these case studies illustrates how extremist groups misuse the concept of "blood debt" to rationalize violence and attract new recruits. The targeted populations may differ, but the underlying rationale—that a "debt" of blood exists and must be repaid through violence—remains the same. Understanding this can be key to countering such extremist narratives effectively.

The Impact: Blood Debt and Global Terrorism

The perversion of the concept of "blood debt" has had wide-reaching and deeply troubling implications for global terrorism. At the most basic level, it supplies an ideological foundation that extremist factions can use to rationalize horrific acts of violence. By claiming that such acts serve to "settle" a blood debt, these groups distort religious teachings to vindicate actions that are not only unethical but also inhumane. This interpretation not only validates the group's violent tactics in the eyes of its followers but also aims to sanctify them, thereby presenting a dangerous distortion of religious texts and principles.

Moreover, the notion of "blood debt" has proven to be a highly effective recruiting tool for extremist groups. In an age of digital media and global connectivity, this skewed concept has transcended geographical and cultural barriers to infiltrate communities far removed from the original theaters of conflict.

For example, extremist propaganda often taps into broader grievances—such as perceptions of Western imperialism or mistreatment of Muslims worldwide—to claim that a collective "blood debt" exists that Muslims everywhere are obligated to settle. This globalizes the local grievances and specific instances that may have initially given rise to the concept, creating a self-perpetuating cycle of recruitment and violence that is increasingly difficult to contain. By making blood debt a part of their ideological toolkit, extremist groups are not only able to incite violence on a global scale but also forge alliances with like-minded groups and individuals worldwide, thereby amplifying the reach and impact of their campaigns.

Challenges and Strategies in Counteracting Extremist Interpretations

Combating the extremist interpretation of the concept of "blood debt" is a formidable challenge that demands a comprehensive, multi-faceted approach. One critical component is education. It is vital to provide a balanced and nuanced understanding of religious teachings, so that extremist groups cannot monopolize religious narratives. This could involve bolstering mainstream religious education to include perspectives that counteract extremist views, thereby neutralizing the ideological breeding grounds that extremist factions exploit. Schools, colleges, and religious institutions can be important allies in this effort, providing platforms for the dissemination of counter-narratives that emphasize the ethical and legal boundaries of concepts like "blood debt" within mainstream religious teachings.

Community-based interventions also have a significant role to play. Local leaders, families, and social organizations can be mobilized to identify and counteract extremist indoctrination at an early stage. By building strong, resilient communities that are educated about the risks of extremist ideology, it becomes harder for extremist groups to recruit new members. Moreover, theological counter-narratives should be developed and promoted. Religious leaders and scholars who command respect within communities can be powerful voices against extremist interpretations. They can present well-reasoned, scripture-based arguments to delegitimize the flawed ideological constructs that groups use to justify violence.

Lastly, it is imperative that governmental bodies and international organizations take an active role in this ideological battle. Collaboration is needed in order to tackle the foundational issues that render extremist ideologies appealing—factors like political volatility, economic hardship, and social inequality. This may require diplomatic negotiations to mediate disputes, development schemes to alleviate poverty and broaden opportunities, as well as community programs aimed at reducing the social stigmatization and exclusion of targeted groups. Such steps can erode the attraction of extremist philosophies, including distorted takes on notions like "blood debt," thus making recruitment and operations increasingly problematic for radical organizations. Ultimately, the task of mitigating extremist interpretations is a long-haul endeavor that calls for the unified efforts of a wide spectrum of stakeholders, from local communities to international bodies.

Chapter 8:
Suicide Bombers - The Complexity of Labeling in War

In the vast tapestry of modern warfare, where the frontlines are as much ideological as they are physical, the very language we use to describe acts of violence becomes a battlefield in itself. The labels we choose carry weight, evoking emotions, signaling alliances, and even justifying further actions. Yet, in this dynamic landscape, few designations prove as contentious and loaded as those related to acts of individual martyrdom or destruction: the suicide bomber.

In this exploration of how we define participants in armed conflicts, we confront a complex set of questions. Are these individuals' mere tools for destruction, or are they guided by political or ideological agendas that extend beyond immediate acts of violence? Navigating the murky confluence of geopolitics, ethics, and language, the aim here is to shed light on the intricate complexities involved in naming such actors. This discussion also challenges readers to contemplate the far-reaching impact of the terminology we choose when addressing matters related to war.

The Dual Challenge of Terminology

In today's volatile landscape of global conflict, the task of labeling, particularly when it zeroes in on figures as controversial as suicide bombers, presents an intricate web of challenges that span linguistic, ethical, and geopolitical domains. The term 'weapon', rooted in antiquity, straightforwardly denotes a tool or apparatus designed explicitly for harm or destruction. This clarity, however, starts to blur when we compare this understanding against the role of a suicide bomber. Without a doubt, the explosive or destructive device that such an individual bears aligns seamlessly with the concept of a weapon. Yet, the individual themself, as the bearer and deployer of this device, functions more as a vessel or medium, complicating their categorization as a mere 'weapon'.

As we further wade into the murky waters of conflict terminology, we encounter the heavily charged term: "terrorist". Originating from acts meant to terrorize or instill profound fear within large populations, the term has evolved to encompass actions often driven by political, religious, or ideological motivations. On the surface, the motivations and actions of a suicide bomber seem to fit together with this understanding, rendering the label of "terrorist" seemingly apt. However, herein lies the crux of the complexity. The term 'terrorist' is not a monolithic, universally accepted label. It is steeped in layers of subjectivity, influenced by socio-political contexts and individual or collective biases. Depending on one's vantage point, cultural background, or political allegiance, a figure labeled a "terrorist" in one narrative could be hailed as a "hero", "martyr", or "freedom fighter" in another.

Adding another layer of intricacy is the ever-evolving nature of warfare itself. As the lines between combatants and civilians blur in asymmetric wars, and non-state actors play increasingly prominent roles, the traditional frameworks for categorization are continually challenged. Thus, the act of labeling becomes less about the objective definitions and more about the interplay of power dynamics, propaganda, perception, and deeply ingrained biases. This exploration, then, is not merely an academic or linguistic endeavor; it is a deep dive into the socio-political undercurrents that shape our understanding of modern conflict.

Context Matters: The Setting of Violent Acts

Understanding the influence of location on acts of violence is not merely a geographic exercise but a deeply analytical one, intertwined with history, geopolitics, and societal norms. Traditional war zones, demarcated by borders and driven by state agendas, come with their own set of established conventions. These conventions, formulated over decades of international dialogue and conflict experiences, provide a semblance of order, laying down rules that parties generally agree to adhere to. Such environments, while chaotic and destructive, offer a semblance of predictability when trying to interpret acts of violence, including those perpetrated by suicide bombers.

However, the narrative experiences a seismic shift when the venue of violence moves away from these recognized battlegrounds. As one delves into acts committed in spaces of daily life – the hustle and bustle of marketplaces, the sanctity of educational institutions, or the peaceful aura of religious sites – the act of a suicide bombing is viewed through an entirely different lens. These are places where children learn, where families bond, and where everyday individuals live out their mundane yet cherished routines. An act of violence here is not just an act against combatants, but a grievous assault on the collective psyche of a community or nation. In these contexts, labels like "terrorist" gain potency, underscoring the violation of spaces typically detached from direct warfare. The rationale behind such strong labels stems from international accords such as the Geneva Conventions, which, while acting as the bedrock of warfare ethics, expressly denounce targeting civilians as not just unlawful but morally reprehensible.

Yet, as with many aspects of modern conflict, there exists a gray area. Asymmetric warfare, a form of conflict where power dynamics are skewed and where the actors often include non-state entities, muddies the waters. In this setting, distinctions become fluid, and labels can become interchangeable. Non-state actors, insurgent groups, and guerrilla fighters might not align with, or even recognize, established conventions. Their motivations, driven by ideology, disenfranchisement, or resistance against perceived oppressors, add layers of complexity to the interpretation of their violent acts. Within this shadowy expanse, understanding the "why" behind an act of violence becomes as crucial, if not more so, than the "where." The larger question becomes: in our quest to label and understand, are we considering the myriad factors that shape these acts, or are we confined by the boundaries of our own perspectives?

The Personal Dimension of Suicide Bombers

While political discussions, ethical quandaries, and legal dissections dominate discourse, the intimate stories of those who become suicide bombers often linger in obscurity. Yet, to truly fathom this phenomenon, we must humanize these individuals, understanding them not just as mere statistics or faceless adversaries, but as complex human beings woven from experiences, emotions, and influences.

Each suicide bomber represents a distinct narrative, a culmination of choices and circumstances that led them to an unimaginable crossroads. War-torn landscapes, with their constant barrage of devastation, bereavement, and instability, serve as crucibles where a myriad of pressures meld together. Firstly, the formidable force of ideological indoctrination cannot be underestimated. Militant groups and extremist ideologies often present the act of self-sacrifice as the pinnacle of heroism, a direct passageway to eternal rewards, or a potent statement against perceived enemies. This potent narrative can seduce individuals, offering them a sense of purpose, belonging, or transcendence in a chaotic world.

However, the psychological strains inherent in such volatile environments play a significant role as well. The traumas of war, witnessing atrocities, losing loved ones, and experiencing personal violations can push individuals to the brink. For some, becoming a suicide bomber might be perceived as reclaiming control in an otherwise powerless existence, or perhaps as a desperate bid for escape from relentless internal and external turmoil.

Socio-economic considerations further complicate the picture. In areas suffocated by poverty, lack of education, and dwindling opportunities, the prospect of financial security for a bomber's family can become a decisive factor. Some extremist groups exploit these vulnerabilities, offering significant sums to the families of those who carry out suicide missions. When such monetary allurements intersect with ideological and psychological pressures, the pull can become irresistible for individuals feeling trapped by circumstance.

Additionally, there is a darker, even more tragic dimension to consider. Not all suicide bombers act entirely of their own volition. Cases abound of individuals who were manipulated, brainwashed, or coerced. Some are even forcibly conscripted into these deadly missions, their autonomy stripped away, turned into mere pawns in larger, sinister games of power and terror.

In our quest to understand this harrowing phenomenon, we must grapple with these multifaceted realities. Behind the act, behind the explosion, there lies a life—a human being shaped by a convergence of factors, many of which are born from the tragedies and complexities of our modern world. And as we seek solutions or responses, this human dimension must always be at the forefront of our considerations.

Navigating the Labyrinth of Labels

At the heart of modern warfare lies a profound paradox: the more technologically advanced and interconnected our world becomes, the murkier the waters of definition and distinction grow. The endeavor to classify a suicide bomber in a war zone as either a "weapon" or a "terrorist" serves as a prime testament to this complexity. It is akin to navigating a labyrinth of labels, where every turn, every decision point, is shaped by a multitude of factors—ranging from geopolitical considerations to personal narratives, from historical legacies to emerging threats.

While the term "weapon" traditionally insinuates an object or tool employed to inflict harm, when applied to a person, the waters of morality and ethics become muddied. Can a human being, with emotions, beliefs, and desires, be simply reduced to an inanimate tool of destruction? Conversely, the term "terrorist" is laden with layers of political, social, and historical implications, all of which might change based on the beholder's viewpoint. Today's terrorist could very well be tomorrow's martyr or freedom fighter, depending on the narratives that gain traction.

Adding to this intricate web are the shifting battlefields of the 21st century. Gone are the days when wars were largely fought in trenches or open fields; today's conflicts can erupt in marketplaces, schools, or even in the intangible realms of cyberspace. Within such arenas, acts of violence take on different connotations, shaped by the context and environment they unfold within.

The Geneva Conventions, while attempting to provide clarity and codification, sometimes struggle to encompass the vast array of acts and actors in modern asymmetric warfare. Non-state actors, guerrilla fighters, and insurgent factions, all operating beyond the traditional purview of state armies, further complicate the equation.

Yet, amidst these macro considerations, one must not lose sight of the micro narratives—the personal stories, dreams, and tragedies of the individuals who become embroiled in these acts. Behind each label, there is a story, often one of manipulation, desperation, or ideological fervor.

To truly understand this intricate dance of labels and acts, one must be prepared to delve deep, to question established norms, and to grapple with ambiguity. It is a journey that requires patience, empathy, and a willingness to embrace the shades of grey that dominate the modern tapestry of war.

Chapter 9:
Terror Within: Attacks on Educational Institutions in the United States

An additional topic that falls under the label of "terrorism" is school shootings. In the American tapestry, educational institutions have always been revered as sanctuaries of enlightenment, growth, and community bonding. Their hallways echo with aspirations, dreams, and the hustle of students preparing to shape the future. However, over recent decades, a cloud of dread has cast its shadow over these institutions, as an alarming frequency of violent acts has disrupted the safety they once promised. No longer just centers of academic pursuit, schools have increasingly found themselves on the front lines of societal turmoil and individual vendetta.

In exploring the troubling phenomenon of school shootings, we find that some incidents are fueled by broader socio-political motives, while many others have their origins in personal issues, frustrations, and mental health challenges. The unsettling intersection of readily available firearms, societal stressors, and various other contributing factors has led to the dire prevalence of these tragic events. The discussion aims to traverse this painful terrain, examining the complex array of underlying causes, the harrowing episodes themselves, and their lasting impact on the collective consciousness of America.

Historical Overview

Schools, long considered pillars of communal gathering and enlightenment, have also, unfortunately, been occasional sites of violence and discord. The annals of American history record such acts of aggression dating back to as early as the 1760s. The most harrowing of these early events occurred when a student took the life of his teacher in front of an assembly, permanently scarring the collective memory of that community. Such incidents, though shocking, were sporadic and far between during these early days. However, as the nation progressed, with its sociopolitical upheavals and evolving cultural landscapes, schools began to mirror these changes in darker ways.

The disturbing increase in violent acts within educational institutions, which reignited in the latter part of the 20th century and has continued into the early 21st century, cannot be ignored. Far from isolated incidents driven by individual grievances, these episodes have escalated in terms of scale, frequency, and intensity. The contributing factors span societal concerns, individual frustrations, and occasionally even geopolitical tensions. This conversation aims to document this unsettling transformation by illuminating the diverse elements that have fueled such a dark evolution.

Notable Incidents

Columbine High School (1999): A watershed moment in the history of American school shootings, two teenagers orchestrated a meticulously planned attack on their peers, claiming 13 lives. The brutality, combined with the attackers' suicides, plunged the nation into a period of soul-searching.

Sandy Hook Elementary School (2012): In Newtown, Connecticut, a lone gunman took the lives of 20 young children and six adult staff members. The sheer youth of the victims intensified the nation's grief and outrage.

Stoneman Douglas High School (2018): A former student of this Parkland, Florida school unleashed a hail of bullets, extinguishing 17 lives. The tragedy reignited fervent nationwide protests and a renewed push for gun control measures.

Robb Elementary School (2022): On May 24, 2022, the Uvalde, Texas community faced a tragic event when 18-year-old former student, Salvador Ramos, shot and killed 19 students and two teachers at Robb Elementary School. The assault reignited national debates on gun violence, culminating in the passage of the Bipartisan Safer Communities Act—a significant piece of federal gun reform legislation.

Underlying Causes

In the distressing landscape of violent attacks within educational institutions, an intricate web of underlying causes emerges, weaving together multiple dimensions of societal, personal, and institutional challenges. At the heart of this maze lies the omnipresent issue of mental health. Historically, many of those who perpetrate these devastating acts have shown signs of psychological distress, hinting at deeper, untreated traumas or disorders. The contemporary mental health infrastructure, though evolving, often falls short of meeting the comprehensive needs of these individuals, leaving many to grapple with their struggles in solitude. This void of support can, tragically, make the descent into violent tendencies swifter and more pronounced.

Another layer adding to is the complexity of America's relationship with firearms, it is essential to acknowledge the country's unique historical connection to guns. The U.S. Constitution's Second Amendment, which enshrines the right to bear arms, consistently sparks impassioned debates. In the real world, this constitutional right can inadvertently simplify the route for those—even with malevolent designs—to acquire weapons lawfully. Moreover, the ease with which firearms can be illegally procured adds another layer of concern. This accessibility, placed alongside unaddressed psychological struggles, creates a volatile mix with the potential for grave consequences.

Equally pressing is the role of social dynamics in molding an individual's worldview and actions. Bullying, ostracization, and the gnawing pain of persistent isolation have been recurring themes in the personal histories of many perpetrators. These experiences, when left unaddressed, can fester, morphing into deep-seated resentments that have the ability to manifest violently. This potential trajectory underscores the urgent need for improvement of the social support systems found within educational settings, aiming to foster inclusion and address grievances proactively.

The media's role in this topic cannot be understated. In the media's race for sharing breaking news stories, the coverage of school shootings can sometimes veer into the sensational. Detailed portrayals of the assailant, their motivations, and the act itself might inadvertently place them on a pedestal of infamy. This unintentional glorification poses risks, potentially inspiring others who, driven by a myriad of motivations, might see violence as a path to similar recognition.

The Response

Amid an era of unsettling events, the nation's educational establishments have been compelled to reevaluate and bolster their protective measures. Historically, educational institutions stood as beacons of knowledge, safety, and personal development. However, recent threats have catalyzed the need for drastic enhancements in security. Schools, once characterized by open doors and welcoming hallways, now often resemble fortresses, equipped with metal detectors meticulously screening entrants, reinforced perimeter fencing hindering the ability to climb, intricate surveillance systems monitoring every nook and cranny, and on-site security officers patrolling grounds to ensure the safety of students and staff alike.

Yet, the response goes beyond just physical security. The mental and emotional well-being of students has been thrust into the spotlight. With an increasing number of attackers displaying histories of psychological distress, schools have recognized the paramount importance of mental health. Institutions, both primary and secondary, are channeling unprecedented resources towards counseling services. This is not merely a reactionary measure; by initiating early interventions, they aim to identify and assist distressed students, potentially diverting them from a path of violence.

The gun control debate, always a fiery topic in the U.S., has been further ignited by these incidents. While the national conversation remains divisive, certain states have taken actions. For example, efforts have been made to strengthen background check systems and to limit the sale of firearms to individuals with known mental health issues or previous violent histories. On the flip side, if legal acquisition becomes tougher due to regulations, some individuals might be pushed to seek firearms through illegal channels. This could increase the demand and profitability of illegal gun sales. Furthermore, in the wake of recent school shootings, communities have become more vigilant, reporting suspicious activities more frequently. This community vigilance can make illegal firearm transactions riskier and more difficult.

Lastly and perhaps the most visceral response, has been the introduction of active shooter drills in schools. These drills, though somber and at times controversial, are designed to provide students and staff with the tools and tactics that could increase their chances of survival during an attack. Regularly conducted, they serve as stark reminders of the times but also as crucial preparatory exercises. While we hope these skills are never called upon, the emphasis is on ensuring everyone is as prepared as possible for any eventuality.

Why Not Labelled as Terrorism???

The debate around labeling school shootings as acts of terrorism touches upon intricate nuances and definitions embedded within legal, political, and media landscapes. Fundamentally, "terrorism" is often defined as acts of violence aiming to instill fear in a population for political, ideological, religious, or social objectives. This characterization underscores intent beyond the act itself, highlighting larger societal or geopolitical ambitions.

By contrast, the majority portion of school shootings in America emerges from personal disputes, mental health issues, or individual vendettas, rather than broader political or ideological motivations. These tragic events undoubtedly wreak havoc and fear within communities, yet they frequently do not possess the strategic aims that are typically associated with terrorism.

The media, with its considerable influence on public perception, exercises caution in its terminology. Mislabeling an event can not only mislead the public but might inadvertently ascribe to the perpetrator a political or ideological weight they neither intended nor claimed. Moreover, the portrayal of school shooters as "terrorists" could inadvertently legitimize their acts as having broader societal motivations or implications, thereby distorting public understanding of the root causes of such events.

Extensive analysis conducted of mass shootings underscores the complexity of this issue. Nearly half of such events studied could be framed as acts of terrorism; however, they were not labeled as such. This speaks volumes about the criteria and interpretations that influence the categorization of such violent events.

Internationally, the distinction between acts rooted in personal motivations and terrorism is widely recognized and is not solely an American anomaly. However, this distinction is a topic of ongoing debate. Many argue that the terror experienced by victims and witnesses of school shootings is on par with that of ideologically-driven acts of terrorism. The distinction, they argue, might appear academic or semantic to those directly affected.

The escalating frequency of school shootings underscores a pressing societal challenge. While the terminology debate is significant, so too is the broader conversation about prevention and response. The American discourse around this issue continuously grapples with the challenge of reconciling foundational American rights with the paramount need to ensure the safety of its students. As the nation seeks solutions, both in policy and societal reform, the semantics, though crucial, form just one facet of a complex issue.

Chapter 10:
Women in Terrorism - Roles, Motivations, and Impact

The conversation about terrorism is frequently framed within a male-centric viewpoint, but recent shifts challenge this established narrative. An increasing number of females are becoming active participants in the world of global terrorism, their roles far exceeding mere footnotes. This trend significantly alters traditional perceptions and adds new dimensions to our understanding of extremist activities. While much about terrorism still relies on long-standing tactics and motivations, the growing involvement of women introduces additional complexities.

No longer are they merely bystanders or passive supporters; women are now front-line operatives, strategic recruiters, and pivotal influencers, actively participating in and often orchestrating acts of terror. Their motivations to join such groups can be as varied as the roles they assume, ranging from personal vendettas to deep-seated ideological convictions. Moreover, the impact they wield is profound. The participation of women in terror activities often captures disproportionate media attention, magnifying the psychological impact of their actions. But beyond the headlines, they also influence the inner dynamics of the terror groups they join, often serving as bridges for recruitment and propagating extremist ideologies.

By delving deeper into the world of women in terrorism, we begin to understand the nuanced interplay of gender, power, and violence, offering a more comprehensive method through which to view and counteract the global challenge of terrorism.

Women as Operatives: From Perpetrators to Suicide Bombers

Historically, women's roles within terrorist organizations were perceived as being on the periphery - often limited to providing logistical support, offering shelter, or disseminating propaganda. However, as the landscape of terrorism metamorphosed, so did the roles of women within its nexus. Their shift from the backdrop to the limelight has been both strategic and alarming. This evolution has not just been about increased participation; it has been about the nature of that participation itself.

From the tumultuous times of political revolutions to the present-day jihadi movements, women have graduated from being mere facilitators to direct actors in terror plots. Their involvement now spans a gamut of activities, from planning and coordination to execution. One of the most potent symbols of this shift is the rise of female suicide bombers. Previously unimaginable, these women, often driven by a potent mix of personal trauma and ideological conviction, have been deployed in many high-profile attacks across the globe. Their choice as suicide bombers is not coincidental; terrorist organizations often exploit societal perceptions of women as non-threatening, enabling them to bypass security measures more easily. Moreover, the societal shock and media attention following a female-led attack often amplifies the psychological impact of such events.

Diverse motivations propel these women into the fore of terror activities. For some, it is personal – revenge for a loved one lost in conflict or counter-terrorism operations. For others, it is ideological – a profound belief in the cause and a desire to be more than just bystanders. At times, it is a combination of coercion and conviction, where personal vulnerabilities are exploited for recruitment, only to later morph into a deeper ideological commitment.

Examining individual instances, such as the involvement of the Black Widows in Chechnya or the role of female members in Boko Haram, we aim to offer a nuanced portrayal of the evolving role of women in terrorist activities. Their journeys, while diverse, share common threads that help us understand why they transitioned from being on the sidelines to becoming engaged actors in acts of terror. Grasping this shift is more than acknowledging their involvement; it calls for a rethinking of our counter-terrorism approaches to adapt to an ever-changing landscape of threats.

The Role of Women as Recruiters and Supporters

Terrorist organizations, like any other structured entities, require a robust network of facilitators and promoters to maintain momentum and expand their influence. Within this paradigm, women have emerged as key players in driving recruitment and ensuring the longevity of these extremist movements. Their roles, often shrouded in subtlety, range from overt recruitment drives to discreet sustenance of communication lines, logistics, and morale.

Women recruiters often leverage social and psychological insights to attract potential new members. They can exploit emotional vulnerabilities, tapping into feelings of exclusion, loss, or perceived wrongs. Their gender also plays a role, as they may be perceived as more empathetic, trustworthy, or non-threatening, thus allowing them easier access to certain communities or vulnerable individuals. Additionally, in certain cultures or societies, women can interact more freely with other women, opening doors to recruit a demographic that might otherwise be inaccessible to male members of a terrorist group.

Platforms like social media have further amplified the outreach potential for these female recruiters. From the corners of encrypted chat rooms to the public arenas of major social media platforms, they weave narratives that romanticize the cause, targeting especially impressionable minds or those seeking a place to fit in.

Beyond recruitment, women play a critical role in sustaining the very fabric of these extremist organizations. They become channels of communication, couriers of vital information, or caregivers tending to injured militants. In some contexts, they manage safe houses, collect funds, or even aid in the indoctrination of children, ensuring the next generation's radicalization.
However, this involvement of women in supporting roles presents significant challenges for counter-terrorism agencies. Their activities can easily blend into everyday society, making detection harder. Traditional surveillance methods, which may be conditioned to focus on male operatives, might overlook these women, inadvertently providing them a cloak of invisibility.

By examining cases such as the women integral to the Tamil Tigers in Sri Lanka or those playing key roles in ISIS recruitment efforts, the focus is to dissect the intricate involvement of women in terrorist organizations. Gaining insights into their roles and strategies is essential for a thorough understanding of extremist networks, as well as for developing sophisticated counter-terrorism measures that recognize and adapt to this gender dimension.

Motivational Factors: Ideology, Personal Grievances, and Empowerment

In the world of terrorism, the pathways leading women to its gates are as varied as they are complex. While it is tempting to search for a singular explanation, the motivations behind female involvement in terrorism often intertwine personal histories, ideological convictions, and the allure of empowerment in a male-dominated space.

Ideologically, many extremist groups craft narratives that resonate deeply with a particular demographic. Women are no exception. Groups may use religious or political dogmas, presenting them in ways that make adherence seem not just desirable, but imperative for the salvation, liberation, or betterment of their community. The narrative may be tailored to evoke a sense of duty, painting the involvement in the cause as a moral or divine obligation. For some women, this ideological alignment offers a clarity of purpose and a sense of companionship that they might not find elsewhere.

Yet, ideology alone does not paint the full picture. Personal grievances and traumas often act as potent catalysts. Women who have experienced personal loss due to conflict, be it the death of loved ones or displacement from their homes, may view terrorist involvement as a means of payback. Their personal pain becomes enmeshed with the broader grievances of their community, fueling a drive to act. Furthermore, personal experiences of abuse, discrimination, or marginalization can become foundational stones in their path toward radicalization, as they seek avenues for justice, revenge, or simply to voice their anger.

Empowerment, as a motivator, cannot be underestimated. In societies where women's roles may be restricted or predefined, terrorist organizations can paradoxically offer a sense of empowerment. The allure of wielding power, whether it is in the form of a weapon, influence over others, or simply having a voice in strategic decisions, can be profound. For some, this involvement shatters societal norms, allowing them to step out of the shadows of subservience and into roles of authority and significance. The mere act of joining such groups can be seen as a bold statement of defiance against patriarchal norms.

By examining individual stories, it becomes clear that their motivations are complicated. Some are lured by ideology, others are driven by personal vendettas, and many are enticed by the promise of empowerment. Understanding these nuances is crucial in devising strategies to counteract the appeal of extremist groups to women and address the root causes that push them into the arms of terrorism.

Case Studies of Prominent Female Terrorists

Throughout history, several women have left their lasting marks, evolving from mere participants to prominent figures orchestrating and executing significant operations. By examining these individuals and their trajectories, one can garner a deeper understanding for the varied roles, motivations, and tactics that characterize women's involvement in terrorism.

Ulrike Meinhof: As one of the co-founders of the German far-left Red Army Faction (RAF), Meinhof's journalistic background provided a unique platform from which to propagate extremist ideologies. Her writings and advocacy played a key role in legitimizing and amplifying the group's agenda. Her journey from journalist to terrorist underscores the interplay between ideology and activism, and how personal convictions can escalate into radical actions.

Samantha Lewthwaite: Dubbed the 'White Widow', Lewthwaite is one of the Western world's most wanted terrorism suspects. Initially coming into the limelight due to her marriage to one of the 7/7 London bombers, she later became affiliated with Somalia's Al-Shabaab. Reports suggest she was involved in orchestrating numerous attacks in East Africa. Her story highlights the global nature of terrorism and underscores how individuals from seemingly contrasting backgrounds can be drawn into its vortex.

Wafa Idris: Recognized as the first female suicide bomber of the Al-Aqsa Intifada, Idris's act in Jerusalem in 2002 marked a pivotal moment in the Palestinian-Israeli conflict. Her background as a paramedic and her personal traumas, including her inability to bear children due to a gunshot wound, provide a glimpse into the complex tapestry of motivations that drive individuals to such acts.

Dzhennet Abdurakhmanova: At just 17, Abdurakhmanova became the face of the Moscow metro bombings in 2010. Hailing from Dagestan, her journey into terrorism was deeply intertwined with personal loss, as her husband – an Islamist militant – was killed in an encounter with Russian forces. Her story accentuates how personal vendettas, interwoven with broader regional conflicts, can fuel radicalization.

Each of these women, drawn from diverse backgrounds and ideologies, underscores the spectrum of roles and motivations that characterize female participation in terrorism. Their stories highlight the transformation of personal grievances and convictions into acts of violence, challenging the conventional narratives of women as passive participants in the world of extremist violence.

Gendered Approaches to Counter-terrorism and Prevention

Addressing the nuanced involvement of women in terrorism requires an understanding that goes beyond traditional counter-terrorism methodologies. Recognizing and incorporating gender dynamics into these strategies is not merely a matter of inclusivity; it is a requisite for effectiveness.

Firstly, it is essential to grasp that women operatives often present unique challenges for detection. Historically conditioned biases may lead security forces to underestimate or overlook women as potential threats, enabling them to exploit these biases to further clandestine operations. Therefore, training and awareness programs need to dismantle pre-existing stereotypes, equipping security personnel with the tools to identify and counter female operatives without bias.

Moreover, preventive strategies tailored for women are crucial. Such strategies must consider socio-cultural contexts, addressing specific issues like gender-based violence or economic disparities that might push women towards extremism. Community-based programs that empower women, offering them education, employment opportunities, and a voice in local governance, can serve as powerful deterrents against radicalization.

Rehabilitation and reintegration programs for female ex-extremists require special attention. Such programs should be designed considering the specific traumas and challenges faced by women in extremist settings. For instance, women might have experienced sexual violence or been forced into marriages. Thus, psychological counseling, socio-economic support, and community engagement are pivotal in ensuring these women successfully transition into mainstream society.

Moreover, addressing the narratives that draw women to extremist ideologies is imperative. This involves challenging and reshaping the notions of empowerment and agency that terrorist organizations might offer to women. Counter-narratives should promote positive role models, showcasing women who have made impactful contributions to society without resorting to violence.

Lastly, collaboration with women's rights organizations can be instrumental. These groups, often rooted deeply in communities, possess insights into local gender dynamics and can guide the design and implementation of gender-sensitive counter-terrorism strategies.

The multifaceted involvement of women in extremist movements, whether as active participants or influential supporters, reiterates the need to understand and address terrorism from all angles. Their motivations, often a blend of ideological, personal, and empowerment-driven factors, demand a nuanced analysis to devise effective prevention and de-radicalization strategies.

Chapter 11:
Environmental Terrorism - Nature, Motivations, and Responses

Environmental terrorism represents a niche yet potent strand of extremism, rooted in the deep-seated belief that dramatic, and at times violent, actions are necessary to draw attention to ecological degradation, halt environmental harm, or promote a more sustainable coexistence with nature. Born from the intersection of environmental advocacy and radical action, this form of terrorism stems from a combination of despair at the accelerating a perceived environmental crises and frustration with traditional activism's supposed ineffectiveness.

At its core, the motivation behind environmental terrorism is viewed as a noble cause by some whom have tasked themselves with safeguarding the planet. Yet, adopted tactics can range from sabotage of infrastructure to targeted attacks against entities perceived as environmental despoilers. Such actions can lead to significant financial damages, disrupt essential services, and in extreme cases, the loss of life.

The focus here is to unravel the essence of environmental terrorism, beginning with its historical backdrop, tracking its growth, and scrutinizing the ideological underpinnings that inspire this form of extremism. By analyzing a series of key incidents, we aim to illuminate the tactics used and the repercussions that ensue.

Furthermore, we will explore the difficulties countries encounter when grappling with this distinct form of threat. Striking the right equilibrium between acknowledging the genuine grievances of environmental activists and curbing violent activities demands a nuanced approach. Tactics to counter environmental terrorism diverge from those used against traditional terrorist activities. By understanding the environmental issues at the core, governments and organizations can aim to resolve these matters while simultaneously reducing the appeal of extreme actions.

Understanding Environmental Terrorism and Ecoterrorist Groups

Environmental terrorism is not merely an offshoot of traditional environmental activism; it is a manifestation of desperation and radicalism born from witnessing continuous environmental degradation.

Historically, the majority of environmentalists have championed non-violent protest and advocacy. However, as perceived environmental crises deepen and political inaction persists, minority groups of environmentalists believe that a more aggressive stance is essential to bringing about tangible change.

This shift from peaceful advocacy to a willingness to employ violent tactics birthed the notion of "ecoterrorism." At the core of such extremism is the belief that traditional methods of protest are too passive, ineffective, or slow to combat pressing environmental threats. Whether driven by the desire to halt deforestation, combat pollution, or stop animal cruelty, these ecoterrorist factions see violence as a necessary tool in their arsenal.

Several ecoterrorist groups have emerged over the years, each with distinct objectives, targets, and tactics. Two of the most notable groups are the Earth Liberation Front (ELF) and the Animal Liberation Front (ALF). These organizations have, at times, orchestrated acts of sabotage against logging companies, research labs, and other entities perceived as perpetrators of environmental harm. Their modes of operation often entail property destruction, with the rationale that such acts, while damaging, avoid direct harm to human life.

However, it is imperative to note the diversity within ecoterrorist groups. While some factions might strictly adhere to non-harming principles, others might be more amenable to direct confrontations. This varied spectrum of motivations and tactics underscores the complexity of environmental terrorism as a whole.

Motivations: Radical Environmentalism, Anti-Corporate Sentiment, and Eco-Anarchism

Diving deep into the motivations behind environmental terrorism requires peeling back the layers of various ideologies that give fuel to this form of extremism. At the heart of this radicalization lies an intensified form of environmentalism. Radical environmentalists hold an unwavering belief in the sanctity of nature. Unlike mainstream environmentalists, who seek solutions within the existing frameworks, radicals perceive the prevailing systems as inherently flawed and destructive. They argue that incremental change is not enough, advocating for transformative action, even if it requires resorting to violence, to protect Mother Nature.

Parallel to radical environmentalism is a strong anti-corporate sentiment. Multinational corporations, particularly those involved in fossil fuels, logging, mining, and industrial agriculture, are often viewed as the primary culprits behind environmental degradation. These corporations, in the eyes of ecoterrorists, prioritize profit over planet, with their actions leading to deforestation, pollution, and species extinction. As such, targeting these entities through sabotage or direct action becomes a symbolic act, highlighting their perceived destructiveness and trying to halt their operations.

Lastly, eco-anarchism merges ecological concerns with a rejection of state and capitalist systems, viewing both as intrinsically oppressive. Eco-anarchists perceive governmental and economic systems as inherently exploitative, not just of people but of the environment as well. In their view, true environmental preservation can only be achieved by dismantling these oppressive structures. This belief often leads to acts that challenge state authority, disrupt capitalist ventures, and promote a return to a more harmonious coexistence with nature.

By examining historical instances, such as the sabotage of logging equipment by radical environmental groups or the destruction of genetically modified crops by anti-corporate activists, one can trace the trajectory of these motivations. For instance, the infamous arson of Vail Mountain's facilities in 1998 by the Earth Liberation Front was a direct response to perceived corporate encroachment on pristine habitats. Such events provide a tangible manifestation of the ideologies driving environmental terrorism.

Tactics and Targets: Sabotage, Property Damage, and Symbolic Acts

Environmental terrorism, driven by fervent ideologies and goals, employs a spectrum of tactics aimed not just at furthering their cause but also at capturing the public's attention. At one end of this spectrum lies property damage, one of the most common tactics employed. Property damage is often directed at corporations or entities perceived as culprits behind environmental degradation. For instance, machinery used for deforestation might be vandalized, or facilities that house animals for experimentation might be broken into in order to "liberate" the animals.

Sabotage is a step further, often involving coordinated efforts to disrupt operations significantly. This might involve the destruction of pipelines, hacking of corporate databases, or even the release of substances that can temporarily render facilities inoperable. The 1999 arson attack on Vail Mountain ski resort by the Earth Liberation Front, which caused over $12 million in damages, serves as a potent reminder of the lengths some groups will go to counteract what they perceive as environmental injustices.

Beyond physical damage, symbolic acts form an essential component of the ecoterrorist's toolkit. These actions may not cause tangible harm but are designed to send a clear message. Such actions might involve large-scale protests, the hanging of banners in strategic locations, or even publicity stunts that force the media and, by extension, the public to take notice of their cause. One vivid example includes Greenpeace activists scaling the Shard in London in 2013, highlighting the dangers of drilling in the Arctic.

The rationale behind these tactics is multifaceted. For one, these acts are designed to inflict economic harm, making it costlier for corporations to pursue environmentally damaging activities. Secondly, they aim to raise public awareness. In a media-driven age, a single act of eco-sabotage can quickly become headline news, forcing discussions about environmental issues to the forefront. Lastly, for many involved, these acts are an expression of direct action and resistance, a tangible way to combat feelings of helplessness in the face of daunting environmental challenges.

Legal and Ethical Considerations in Dealing with Environmental Terrorism

Environmental terrorism, with its complex intersection of environmentalism and extremist actions, presents a unique set of challenges for legal systems worldwide. To begin with, the legal definitions vary. What one country might classify as a terrorist act, another might view as a legitimate, albeit radical, form of environmental protest. The variations in definitions and the absence of a universally accepted classification can lead to jurisdictional disputes and complexities when these acts cross borders.

Prosecuting ecoterrorist acts adds another layer of complexity. The crimes committed by environmental terrorists, such as sabotage or property damage, are often not motivated by personal gain but by ideological beliefs. This distinction, while clear in the minds of the perpetrators, can blur in the legal arena, making it difficult to apply traditional criminal charges that accurately reflect the nature and severity of the act.

Compounding these legal challenges are ethical considerations. On one hand, there is a clear imperative to protect the environment and appreciate the urgency that drives environmental activists. On the other, there is a need to maintain law and order, ensuring that acts of violence or destruction do not become legitimized means of protest. Striking a balance between these competing priorities requires discernment and empathy.

Furthermore, the methods used by governments and law enforcement agencies to counteract environmental terrorism can sometimes tread a fine line between necessary surveillance and potential infringement on civil liberties. As with all forms of extremism, there is a danger in overreach, where innocent non-violent activists and protestors might find themselves unjustly targeted or profiled, purely based on their association with environmental causes.

Another ethical quagmire is the balance between protecting national interests and economic entities and preserving the environment. For example, should governments prioritize the protection of industries that are frequently targeted by ecoterrorists, such as logging or animal testing facilities? Or should they reassess and potentially modify the practices of these industries to address the underlying environmental grievances?

Addressing Root Causes and Promoting Eco-friendly Solutions

Environmental terrorism did not emerge in a vacuum. Often, its roots can be traced to genuine concerns about the planet's well-being, frustrations over perceived political and corporate apathy, and the sense of urgency stemming from the perceived rapid degradation of the natural environment. Addressing these root causes is paramount to ensuring that radical ideologies do not find fertile ground to grow.

Firstly, failed conservation efforts often serve as catalysts for extremist actions. When well-intentioned policies fail to yield desired results or when they are perceived as mere lip service, it can foster disillusionment among environmental activists. This sentiment can lead some to believe that more drastic measures, beyond peaceful protests or lobbying, are necessary to jump start real change.

Corporate exploitation, too, plays a significant role in fanning the flames of ecoterrorism. In areas where industries wreak havoc on local ecosystems, whether through deforestation, excessive mining, or pollution, communities feel the impact firsthand. When these corporations operate with seeming impunity, it can create a narrative where direct action against these entities appears to be the only viable recourse.

Political inaction is another crucial factor. When governments appear to prioritize economic growth over environmental sustainability or when they are perceived as being in the pockets of major corporations, it creates a fertile ground for radicalization. The lack of robust environmental policies or the lax implementation of existing ones sends a message that the environment is not a priority, pushing some activists towards extremism.

To mitigate these issues, eco-friendly advancements and sustainable practices are imperative. Public and private sectors similarly should be at the forefront of embracing renewable technologies, reducing carbon emissions, and putting a focus on sustaining natural resources. Through proactive engagement with local communities in conservation activities, decision-makers can create more customized and effective strategies that address community-specific needs.

In addition, elevating environmental literacy and consciousness can serve as a conduit between activists and legislative bodies. Creating an informed populace that understands both the challenges and solutions related to environmental conservation can lead to more constructive dialogues and less contentious debates on the subject.

In conclusion, countering environmental terrorism is as much about addressing the tangible issues plaguing our environment as it is about understanding and addressing the psychological and socio-political underpinnings of ecoterrorist behaviors. Confronting environmental terrorism necessitates a delicate dance between upholding legal frameworks and honoring ethical imperatives. It is a topic of discussion that demands nuance, understanding, and a commitment to justice. By recognizing the complexities inherent in this challenge, governments, law enforcement agencies, and society at large can approach the issue of environmental terrorism with the depth and seriousness it warrants.

Chapter 12:
State Actors and Terrorism - Unmasking Hidden Alliances

In the landscape of terrorism, what often appears as the actions of independent, non-state entities actually masks a more complex truth. Hidden behind numerous terrorist activities is a web of connections that sometimes implicates state actors. Delving into the unclear realm of state-sponsored terrorism, we aim to shed light on the relationships that can exist between established governments and extremist groups. By investigating their underlying motivations, strategies, and geopolitical interests, we seek to unravel the enigmatic links between sovereign nations and the extremist entities they may secretly back.

State-sponsored terrorism is not a new phenomenon. Throughout history, countries have leveraged extremist groups as proxies to further their geopolitical aims. Whether providing them with arms, funds, training, or even diplomatic support, states sometimes find it advantageous to have a 'hidden hand' in regional or global conflicts. This covert support is rooted in plausible deniability, where states can advance their objectives without being overtly involved. However, the relationships between state sponsors and their proxy groups are not always straightforward. They are governed by shifting geopolitics, evolving national interests, and the ever-changing landscape of global power dynamics. To truly understand state-sponsored terrorism, one needs to look beyond the apparent chaos and discern the underlying patterns and strategies at play.

Several factors drive states to support extremist groups covertly. First and foremost are geopolitical considerations. By backing certain groups, states can exert influence in regions where they might not have a significant direct presence. This indirect control allows them to shape regional outcomes in their favor.

Additionally, states may support terrorist entities as a countermeasure against rival nations. Through proxy warfare, they can weaken adversaries without engaging in full-blown conflict, making terrorism a tool of asymmetric warfare. Furthermore, internal politics can also play a role. Governments might clandestinely back extremist groups to suppress domestic opposition or to divert public attention from pressing internal issues.

Furthermore, economic motivations should not be overlooked. Control over resources, trade routes, or strategic territories might necessitate the destabilization of certain regions, making extremist groups valuable allies for some states. Lastly, ideological alignment between a state and a terrorist entity can also be a motivating factor, especially if the state believes that the group's activities align with its broader cultural, religious, or ideological goals.

State-Sponsored Terrorism: Historical and Modern Context

Throughout history, the symbiotic relationship between states and terrorist organizations has been a defining feature of global geopolitics. During the Cold War, for instance, superpowers like the United States and the Union of Soviet Socialist Republics (USSR) often channeled funds, arms, and resources to various insurgent and extremist groups to fight proxy wars or destabilize regions. Examples include the American support for the Afghan Mujahideen during the Soviet-Afghan War and the Soviet Union's backing of leftist guerrilla movements in Latin America and Africa.

The Middle East has witnessed several instances of state-sponsored terrorism. Iran's backing of Hezbollah in Lebanon or its ties with Shia militias in Iraq offers insights into how states use such groups to further regional ambitions. Similarly, past connections between Libya under Muammar Gaddafi and various extremist factions, including the Irish Republican Army (IRA), showcased how state sponsorship can span continents.

The modern era has not seen a decline in the ties between states and extremist entities, but rather a shift in dynamics and actors. For instance, North Korea has been accused of supporting various extremist groups and engaging in state-sanctioned acts of terrorism, such as the assassination of Kim Jong-nam, Kim Jong-un's half-brother.

In the turbulent landscape of the Middle East, accusations abound. Syria's Assad regime has been implicated in supporting various factions at different times to serve its interests. Iran's backing of Houthi rebels in Yemen is another modern instance of a state leveraging non-state actors to influence regional dynamics.

Furthermore, Pakistan has faced allegations of supporting or turning a blind eye to various militant groups operating within its borders, which are seen as strategic assets in its rivalry with India. On the other side, India has consistently denied Pakistan's claims of its involvement in supporting separatist movements in Balochistan.

The complexity of state-sponsored terrorism in the modern context is underpinned by cyber warfare. States can now sponsor or endorse cyber-terrorist activities, giving them a new dimension of plausible deniability while causing economic, social, or political havoc in target countries.

Factors Behind State Support for Terrorism

Geopolitical objectives play a paramount role in the international arena, dictating the dynamics between states, their allies, and adversaries. Terrorism can become a potent tool when backed by state resources and intelligence. For nations with geopolitical ambitions that might be impeded by direct military intervention — whether due to international treaties, potential political backlash, or superior military adversaries — supporting terrorist organizations provides a covert avenue to achieve their objectives. For instance, a state might back insurgent groups in resource-rich areas to disrupt a rival nation's access to those resources. Additionally, by promoting instability or supporting opposition groups in rival countries, a state can subtly ensure the ascent of more amicable governments, thus creating a more favorable balance of power. This covert maneuvering allows states to further their geopolitical interests without directly getting their hands dirty, sidestepping international reprisals and retaining their global image.

The complexities of modern geopolitics often mean that direct confrontations between major powers can have wide-ranging, sometimes global, repercussions. This is particularly true in regions with nuclear-armed adversaries or where multiple global powers have vested interests. Herein lies the allure of proxy warfare. Instead of direct conflict, states use third-party actors, often terrorist organizations or insurgent groups, as chess pieces in their grander strategy. These proxies can harass, destabilize, and divert the resources of adversaries, all while the sponsoring state maintains a degree of separation. The fallout of any untoward incident, such as an act that garners international condemnation, can be distanced from the patron state. This plausible deniability, a cornerstone of proxy warfare, ensures that the patron can continue its covert operations with reduced risk of direct retaliation or international sanctions.

Beyond the cold calculations of geopolitics lie the deep-seated affinities based on culture, ethnicity, and ideology. Such affinities can blur the lines between strategic advantage and moral obligation. For instance, a state might feel compelled to support a separatist movement in a neighboring country if they share a common ethnic or cultural bond, viewing their involvement as a moral duty rather than mere strategy. This sentiment can be further intensified if the group faces persecution. On the ideological front, states with shared religious or political ideologies might see each other as natural allies, leading them to support groups that further their shared worldview. This is not just about expanding influence but preserving, propagating, and defending a shared set of beliefs or values. Such motivations, deeply intertwined with national identity and narrative, can lead states to back extremist entities with fervor and commitment, seeing their actions as justified in the grand tapestry of their shared history, culture, or belief system.

Tactics and Techniques of State-Sponsored Terrorism

When states decide to provide direct military or financial support to proxy groups, they often do so with subtlety to maintain a facade of non-involvement. This can range from sending military advisors to train insurgents, deploying special forces in covert operations to bolster the capabilities of the proxies, or even providing close air support under the guise of routine operations. Such direct involvement serves a dual purpose: it enhances the effectiveness of the proxy group, making them a formidable force against adversaries, and it provides the state with a degree of control over the actions and objectives of the group. By embedding elements of their own military within these groups, states can guide their operations in alignment with broader geopolitical strategies and goals.

Financial support remains one of the most common ways states back terrorist entities. With significant funding, these groups can procure advanced weapons, sustain prolonged campaigns, and recruit more extensively. But money is just the tip of the iceberg. States also set up clandestine training camps where recruits of these organizations are schooled in guerrilla warfare, bomb-making, intelligence gathering, and other aspects of modern insurgency.

Furthermore, a state might use its network to funnel arms and equipment to its proxies. This could be done discreetly through third-party arms dealers or by staging "lost" caches for the proxy group to "find." Such support greatly amplifies the capabilities of these groups, enabling them to challenge established military forces or sow significant chaos.

Raw intelligence serves as the cornerstone in contemporary conflicts. When a state furnishes crucial intelligence to non-state entities, it significantly amplifies the operational capabilities of a terrorist organization. This assistance can range from revealing the positions of opposing military units to identifying key targets for attacks, or even offering the technology needed to decode encrypted communications from the enemy.

Moreover, coordinating with these groups allows a state to plan joint operations or ensure that the actions of the proxy align with its own strategic objectives. Through encrypted channels, satellite communication, or covert liaisons, states maintain a line of communication, ensuring that the proxy group's actions further the state's geopolitical goals while minimizing chances of unwanted international incidents.

Case Studies of State-Sponsored Terrorism

Iran's Support for Hezbollah: One of the most cited instances of state-sponsored terrorism is Iran's support for Hezbollah, a Shiite political and military organization in Lebanon. Formed in the 1980s in response to the Israeli occupation of southern Lebanon, Hezbollah quickly received backing from Iran in terms of financial aid, weapons, and training. Both parties share a common Shiite ideology and opposition to perceived Western and Israeli hegemony in the region. Over the years, Hezbollah has grown into a formidable political and military force in Lebanon, with Iran continuing to provide support, allegedly including sophisticated weapons systems. Apart from Hezbollah, Iran has also been backing other militia groups in Iraq, Yemen, and other parts of the Middle East to further its regional ambitions.

Syria's Proxy Militias: The Syrian civil war, which began in 2011, witnessed the Syrian government, led by President Bashar al-Assad, using various proxy militias to bolster its efforts against rebel factions. With the backing of allies like Russia and Iran, Syria employed these groups to extend its reach, reclaim lost territories, and suppress opposition forces. These militias, often sectarian in nature, play a crucial role in the conflict, acting as force multipliers for the Syrian Army and its allies.

Pakistan's Alleged Support for Militant Organizations: Pakistan has frequently been accused, particularly by India and Afghanistan, of supporting or turning a blind eye to various militant organizations operating within its territory. Groups like Lashkar-e-Taiba, which India blames for the 2008 Mumbai attacks, and the Afghan Taliban have allegedly received support or safe haven in Pakistan. Pakistan has routinely denied these allegations, maintaining that it is itself a victim of terrorism. Nonetheless, the intricate relations between some elements of Pakistan's security establishment and certain militant groups continue to be a point of international contention and concern.

North Korea's Provocation and Cyberterrorism Tactics: North Korea, often seen as a rogue state, has been implicated in various acts that bear the hallmarks of state-sponsored terrorism. Apart from conventional provocations, North Korea has been accused of engaging in cyberterrorism. The 2014 hack of Sony Pictures, allegedly in retaliation for a film satirizing North Korean leader Kim Jong-un, is one such example. Additionally, North Korea's covert operations, including the assassination of Kim Jong-nam (Kim Jong-un's half-brother) using a nerve agent in Malaysia in 2017, underscore the regime's willingness to employ extreme measures beyond its borders.

International Response and Diplomatic Challenges

International organizations play a pivotal role in addressing and condemning state-sponsored terrorism. The United Nations, through its Security Council and General Assembly, has often been the epicenter of such efforts, passing resolutions against countries suspected of supporting terrorist activities and establishing committees to monitor and combat terrorism. Moreover, regional bodies like the European Union, the African Union, and the Organization of American States have often taken a stand against state-sponsored terrorism, facilitating dialogue and sometimes mediating between the accused state and the aggrieved parties.

One of the primary tools employed by the international community to deter state sponsorship of terrorism is the imposition of sanctions. These economic and diplomatic measures aim to cripple the offending state's ability to provide support to terrorist organizations. Sanctions can target individual leaders, specific sectors of the economy, or the accused state as a whole.

Furthermore, diplomatic isolation, which involves the severing of diplomatic ties and expulsion of ambassadors, can be employed to send a strong message to states involved in supporting terrorism. These actions, however, can have unintended consequences, affecting the civilian population or driving the accused state further into extremism.

Addressing state-sponsored terrorism poses significant diplomatic challenges. Often, the accused state has strategic or economic importance to major world powers, complicating the response. For instance, while a country might be implicated in supporting terrorism, it might also be a key trading partner, house important military bases, or be pivotal in regional stability. This delicate balancing act forces nations to weigh their counter-terrorism efforts against broader national interests, leading to a nuanced and sometimes inconsistent international response. It underscores the complexities inherent in the global fight against terrorism, where practical politics, economic considerations, and strategic alliances can sometimes overshadow counter-terrorism priorities.

Challenges in Holding State Sponsors Accountable

Establishing concrete evidence of a state's involvement in supporting terrorism is a daunting task. By nature, state-sponsored terrorism is covert, with governments going to great lengths to ensure their actions remain hidden. Intelligence agencies often find it challenging to intercept or decrypt classified communications between state actors and terrorist organizations. Even when evidence is obtained, it might be deemed too sensitive to disclose publicly, as doing so might compromise intelligence sources or methods. Moreover, the line between state support and the actions of rogue elements within the government can be blurry, further complicating the attribution.

State sovereignty, the bedrock upon which the modern international system rests, has long been revered as a safeguard against external interference. Rooted in centuries of political thought and diplomatic practice, this principle endorses the idea that each state is the supreme authority within its borders and ought to remain free from external intervention. However, when this principle collides with the global ambition to counter state-sponsored terrorism, it presents a complex challenge.

In a world where borders and national identities matter immensely, respect for sovereignty is paramount. This respect is enshrined in international law, treaties, conventions, and norms that dictate how nations interact. Sovereignty is not just about physical boundaries; it is about preserving the autonomy, dignity, and agency of a nation-state.

Yet, this very shield of protection can, in certain scenarios, become a cloak of invisibility. When accusations of state-sponsored terrorism arise, the line between protecting a nation's sovereignty and ensuring global security blurs. How can the international community act against a potential threat if it is shielded within the protective shell of sovereignty?

The United Nations Charter, a seminal document that forms the cornerstone of international relations, further complicates this narrative. While it is committed to maintaining international peace and security, it simultaneously champions the sovereignty and equality of its member states. Thus, any move perceived as infringing upon a nation's sovereignty—even if motivated by genuine security concerns—becomes a diplomatic minefield. The Charter's emphasis on non-interference means that states, even when suspected of unsavory activities, can rally behind its provisions to fend off criticism.

Direct interventions, be they military, economic, or political, are always contentious. They invite debates on legitimacy, purpose, and intent. Sovereign states accused of supporting or harboring terrorist entities can often leverage the rhetoric of sovereignty to stymie international scrutiny. By invoking their right to non-interference, they can effectively deflect global censure, painting any accusatory fingers as overreaches or breaches of international decorum.

Furthermore, the intricacies of proving state-sponsored terrorism add another layer of complexity. Given that states rarely leave overt traces of their support to extremist groups, the burden of proof becomes immense. And when evidence is finally gathered, the protective barrier of sovereignty often makes it difficult to act upon.

Enter the International Criminal Court (ICC). Established as a beacon of justice, the ICC is tasked with prosecuting the gravest of international crimes. But its creation, while a significant leap forward, is not a universal remedy for all the ills of international transgressions. Several limitations hamstring the court, especially when it comes to state-sponsored terrorism.

Firstly, the scope of the ICC is confined to its founding document, the Rome Statute. While it covers war crimes, crimes against humanity, and genocide, terrorism—state-sponsored or otherwise—is conspicuously absent. This omission already sets a challenging backdrop when attempting to bring state actors to justice for supporting terrorism.

Moreover, the global reach of the ICC is inherently limited by its membership. Many influential powers, who wield significant sway in international politics, have either not ratified or have openly opposed the Rome Statute. Without these major players on board, the ICC faces a diminished authority, with gaps in its jurisdictional reach.

The ICC's dependence on state cooperation further exacerbates its limitations. Unlike national judicial bodies, the ICC does not possess its own enforcement mechanisms. It can issue arrest warrants, but the actual apprehension and transfer of suspects hinge on the cooperation of individual states. This becomes particularly thorny when the accused hail from powerful nations or are protected by strong allies. The very states implicated in wrongdoing can shield suspects, rendering the ICC's warrants powerless.

Beyond these structural challenges, the tangle of international diplomatic practices throws up additional roadblocks. Diplomatic immunity, a long-standing tenet of international relations, offers protection to a range of state officials from legal processes. This immunity can act as a shield for those involved in unsavory conducts, including the sponsorship of terrorism.

Lastly, political considerations often play an outsized role in international justice. States might be reluctant to act against their allies or might prioritize geopolitical and economic interests over judicial pursuits. As a result, the quest for justice can be derailed by the power plays of international politics.

Preventing and Countering State-Sponsored Terrorism

Countering state-sponsored terrorism is not a task for the weak. It is a complex, multidimensional challenge that demands a response equally intricate in its scope. Central to this response is the powerful and indispensable principle of multilateral cooperation among the global community.

In the vast tapestry of international relations, no thread is more crucial than the binding force of collective action. By banding together, forming international coalitions, and solidifying alliances, nations create an interconnected web of deterrence. This web ensures that rogue states thinking of supporting extremist groups must not only contend with one nation but a united front of many.

This unity is not merely symbolic. Sharing intelligence, an often-guarded commodity, among allies brings forth a wealth of benefits. Every piece of information, no matter how insignificant it may seem alone, can contribute to a clearer picture when combined with others. It is the difference between seeing a few puzzle pieces scattered on a table and viewing the complete image they form when connected. When nations are privy to intelligence about impending threats or suspicious activities, they are better equipped to thwart or mitigate those threats, ensuring the safety of their citizens and maintaining global stability.

But it is not just about information sharing. Joint counter-terrorism exercises, a form of military and strategic planning, underscore the collective might of nations working in tandem. Such exercises simulate real-world scenarios, sharpening the skills and tactics of the involved forces. Moreover, they offer a platform for innovation, where different countries bring unique methodologies, doctrine and technologies to the table. The shared learning from these exercises is invaluable.

Furthermore, hosting multilateral summits serves a dual purpose. On a tactical level, they foster dialogues, setting the stage for strategic planning and cooperation. On a more symbolic level, they represent a show of unity, a powerful tableau of nations standing shoulder to shoulder. For any state considering dabbling in supporting extremist activities, such a display serves as a stark reminder: they are not just up against one country but an entire coalition of determined and likeminded nations.

Economic tools, when wielded correctly, are not just mere instruments for commerce or trade. They can be formidable weapons in the global fight against the dark specter of state-sponsored terrorism. The old saying "money talks" holds especially true here. By deploying sanctions, a powerful tool in any country's arsenal, the international community broadcasts a resounding message: supporting extremist factions will not be tolerated.

But it is not just about sending a message. Sanctions bite, and they can bite hard. They strangle the economic lifelines of a country, making basic necessities like food and fuel scarce and expensive. The ordinary citizen feels the pinch, leading to internal pressures placed on their government. As the coffers run dry, so too does the enthusiasm for clandestinely bankrolling extremist groups.

Next, consider the freezing of assets. It is like slamming the brakes on a speeding car. Suddenly, funds that were easily accessible become untouchable. This abrupt halt can be disastrous for those depending on those funds, especially extremist groups who often rely on a steady stream of income for their operations.

Trade restrictions, too, are a potent tool. Denying a country access to global markets, goods, and services can quickly make the costs of supporting extremist outfits hard to swallow. Trade is a two-way street, and without access to vital imports or profitable exports, a country can find itself economically isolated and vulnerable.

However, there is a broader strategic aspect to this. The international financial system, intricate and vast, plays an unsung role in geopolitics. Restricting access to this network can severely curtail a country's ability to execute financial transactions, making it challenging to both fund and facilitate acts of terror.

Now, imagine the combined might of the global community. Engaging powerhouses like the World Bank, International Monetary Fund, or even influential trade blocs can supercharge these economic countermeasures. It is one thing for a single nation to impose sanctions. It is a whole different ballgame when the international financial community stands united in its resolve. With their collective influence, they can make supporting extremist factions not just costly, but downright ruinous.

The global war against state-sponsored terrorism is more than just a battle of arms and intelligence; it is a battle for trust and truth. In this vast arena, transparency and accountability emerge as twin pillars, holding the weight of global expectations and aspirations.

When states embrace transparency, they do not just open a window into their operations; they send out a powerful message about their intentions. By being candid about foreign policy goals and actions, countries strip away the shadows where clandestine dealings thrive. It is challenging for a state to secretly back extremist factions when its every move is under a lens. Such openness not only deters covert support for terror groups but also bolsters a country's standing in the international community.

But how do we ensure this transparency? The answer lies in the meticulous machinery of international apparatuses. Consider mandatory reports on arms sales or foreign aid disbursements. These reports, if mandated by international treaties or bodies, can act like spotlights, illuminating the often murky pathways of weapon transfers or funds, potentially revealing ulterior motives.

Yet, the state machinery, as vast and intricate as it may be, is not the sole player on this stage. Enter non-governmental organizations (NGOs) and watchdog groups. Independent, often grassroots, and driven by a mission, these entities bring a level of scrutiny that is both relentless and unbiased. Acting as the eyes and ears of the public, they dive into the intricate web of international relations, surfacing with insights, revelations, and sometimes, uncomfortable truths. Their external oversight ensures that no stone remains unturned in the quest to uncover state-sponsored terrorism.

Beyond mechanisms and monitoring, there is the domain of international norms and conventions. These are not just documents; they are covenants that tie nations together under a shared promise. By establishing and universally accepting norms that decry state support for terrorism, the global community creates a culture where accountability is not just expected—it is demanded. Such norms serve as the moral compass guiding state actions.

However, norms and agreements are only as good as their enforcement. This is where periodic reviews and evaluations, facilitated by international bodies, come into play. Like a diligent teacher evaluating a student's performance, these reviews measure a state's actions against its commitments. Any deviation, any breach, does not just result in diplomatic rebukes. It attracts tangible consequences, ensuring nations think twice before sponsoring terrorism.

While state-sponsored terrorism looms as a sinister challenge in the global landscape, the tools of transparency and accountability, when wielded with precision and commitment, can act as powerful counterforces. Together, they weave a fabric of trust, truth, and collective responsibility—one strong enough to halt even the most determined state sponsors of terror in their tracks.

Ethical Dilemmas in Responding to State Sponsors

Responding to state sponsors of terrorism has long been a minefield of ethical dilemmas that cut across various dimensions, most prominently in the domains of diplomacy, civilian impact, and the influence of the digital age's media landscape.

The interplay between counter-terrorism endeavors and diplomatic relations is particularly intricate. As nations stand on the frontlines, defending their citizens and interests against the ominous shadow of state-sponsored terrorism, they are simultaneously embroiled in a complex array of international relationships that must be delicately maintained. A robust response to terrorism, while potentially effective in the short term, risks severing essential diplomatic lifelines, thereby setting the stage for longer-term geopolitical isolation, mutual distrust, and even escalated hostilities. Herein lies the balancing act: Can nations fortify themselves against immediate threats, ensuring the safety of their citizens, without upending the nuanced ballet of international diplomacy?

Yet, even as states grapple with this dichotomy, another ethical challenge looms large— the potential collateral damage borne by innocent civilians. Often, the tools wielded in response to state-sponsored terrorism, whether economic, diplomatic, or military, cast a wide net. Economic sanctions, while aimed at deterring malicious state actors, might inadvertently suffocate an entire nation's economy. The general populace, far removed from the corridors of power and decision-making, can find themselves ensnared in a web of shortages, hyperinflation, and societal unrest.

Similarly, military interventions, though aimed at neutralizing threats, risk the inadvertent loss of civilian lives, leading to displacement, trauma, and a cascade of humanitarian issues. This raises an ethically agonizing conundrum: How do nations navigate this terrain, ensuring both security and the preservation of innocent lives?

Layered atop these challenges is the potent and sometimes volatile influence of digital media. In an era defined by its interconnectedness, where news travels at the speed of light and borders seem more like suggestions, public sentiment, molded and amplified by media, is a force to reckon with. Governments, while recognizing the foundational role of an informed public in democracies, are often at the mercy of this rapid information churn.

Media narratives, particularly in the heat of the moment, might not always reflect the nuanced realities on the ground and can sometimes be tainted by biases or misinformation. The resultant fervor can push administrations toward decisions that resonate with the prevailing public sentiment but might be misaligned with long-term ethical and strategic imperatives. This presents a formidable challenge for leaders: In an age where every action is under the microscope and magnified for the world to see, how do they balance the imperative of public accountability with the equally vital need for deliberate, informed, and ethically sound decision-making?

In summary, the challenges of responding to state-sponsored terrorism necessitate a dance of diplomacy, an unwavering commitment to ethical considerations, and a keen understanding of the power and pitfalls of digital-age media. As the world grows ever more interconnected, the stakes, intricacies, and ethical nuances of this challenge will only amplify.

The Future Landscape of State-Sponsored Terrorism

The fluid nature of global politics, underpinned by ever-changing alliances, rivalries, and power struggles, has had profound implications for the strategies states deploy in pursuit of their geopolitical ambitions. Among the most intriguing and concerning shifts in this landscape has been the evolving character of state-sponsored terrorism. Historically, states have been observed lending support primarily to ethno-nationalist factions or groups bound by shared ideologies. This support was rooted in a confluence of interests, where both the state and its proxy saw mutual benefit in their partnership. However, the modern era, with its complex geopolitical challenges, has ushered in a more diverse set of actors on this stage.

One of the most notable manifestations of this shift has been the increasing reliance on mercenary outfits. Distinct from ideologically motivated groups, these mercenaries operate in a transactional environment. Bereft of any deep-rooted ideological commitment, they are mostly swayed by monetary incentives, making them malleable instruments in the hands of ambitious states. Their ability to operate under various banners, coupled with a willingness to switch allegiances based on the promise of better rewards, presents state actors with opportunities to execute covert operations with an enhanced degree of deniability.

Yet, the evolution in state-sponsored activities is not confined to the shadows of covert military operations. The tapestry of the global economy, interwoven with intricate supply chains, financial interdependencies, and shared technological platforms, has become an arena for statecraft and subterfuge. Recognizing the vulnerabilities inherent in this interconnectedness, states have begun to employ non-conventional means of economic disruption. By deploying proxy actors, they aim to hamstring their adversaries' economic machinery, disrupt crucial supply chains, or manipulate market dynamics in ways that can destabilize entire economies.

This broadening of the playbook is emblematic of the rise of 'hybrid warfare', a strategy that melds traditional military tactics with unconventional and often covert operations. In this approach, states harness a combination of conventional forces, irregular troops, cyber campaigns, and economic tactics. The use of proxies in such endeavors offers a veil of obfuscation, allowing states to maintain a level of distance and deniability. The intention is clear: achieve strategic objectives, weaken adversaries, and tilt the balance of power in one's favor without resorting to overt military confrontations that could escalate into full-blown wars.

The rapid advancement of technology has given rise to a new domain of state-sponsored terrorism: cyber warfare. Rather than relying solely on physical attacks, states can now deploy cyber terrorists to infiltrate, sabotage, and spy on target nations. This includes activities like hacking critical infrastructure (e.g., power grids, water supply systems), espionage, disseminating misinformation, and disrupting communication networks. Given its stealthy nature, cyber warfare offers states plausible deniability, making it a particularly appealing tactic. Moreover, with the increasing dependence on Artificial Intelligence and Internet of Things (IoT) devices, the potential avenues for cyber-attacks and their consequent impacts are only set to grow.

The mutable nature of state-sponsored terrorism means that nations need to remain vigilant and adaptive. As states evolve in their tactics, counter-terrorism efforts must also adapt. We can anticipate the rise of multi-domain operations, where states coordinate activities across land, sea, air, space, and cyberspace. There is also a likelihood of states exploiting social divides in target countries, stoking unrest through misinformation campaigns or supporting divisive extremist groups.

To counter these threats, international cooperation will be paramount. This involves not only intelligence sharing but also joint technological development to safeguard critical infrastructures, collaborative diplomatic efforts to sanction rogue states, and fostering global norms against the support for terrorism. The future landscape demands a proactive, unified, and dynamic approach to anticipate and counter state-sponsored terror threats.

Chapter 13:
Terrorist Financing - Follow the Money Trail

Behind every act of terrorism lies a complex web of financial transactions that sustains and supports these illicit activities. These are not just mere transactions; they form the very lifeblood that enables terror groups to recruit, arm and supply themselves, train, and execute their nefarious plots. To further understand the persistence and resilience of these organizations, one must delve deep into the mechanics of their financial dealings.

In this analysis, we delve into the comprehensive world of terrorist financing. The revenue streams that fuel these extremist activities are diverse, ranging from state backing and ransom payments to organized crime. They also include subtler avenues such as money laundering, crowdfunding, and cryptocurrency transactions. Yet, identifying these financial sources is only part of the challenge. The global community, fully aware of the pivotal role that funding plays in sustaining terrorism, has united in efforts to cut off these lifelines. These collective actions include sharing intelligence across borders, implementing strict banking protocols, and zeroing in on economic centers and middlemen who may unwittingly facilitate these transactions.

As financial systems grow increasingly complex, the tactics employed by terrorists to secure funding also adapt, resulting in an ongoing, challenging chase. This exploration not only shines a light on the intricate financial networks that fuel terrorism but also highlights the unceasing, cooperative efforts on a global scale aimed at unraveling them. The saying "follow the money" remains especially relevant, serving as a key battleground in the fight against international extremism.

The Importance of Financial Networks for Terrorist Operations

Terrorism, in its many manifestations, is underpinned by intricate financial operations that extend across global landscapes, interweaving conventional banking systems, underground networks, and innovative financial instruments. At the very core of any terrorist operation lies its funding mechanism. It is akin to the circulatory system in the human body, pumping resources, and ensuring vitality to every nook and cranny of the organization. These financial networks are not just mere channels for money; they provide terrorist entities with the ability to recruit fresh blood, radicalize individuals, strategize operations, purchase sophisticated weaponry, and materialize their ominous objectives.

Delving deeper, the historical trajectory of these financial strategies reveals an evolutionary saga. As the global community has honed its counter-terrorism tactics, especially financial intelligence and enforcement mechanisms, terrorist groups have concurrently revamped their modus operandi. Their approaches to funding have metamorphosed over the decades, reflecting an agile adaptability to the global crackdown on their monetary lifelines. Whereas yesteryears might have seen them heavily reliant on overt acts like bank heists or state sponsorship, the modern terrorist financier operates with a blend of brazenness and discretion. Kidnappings for ransoms still remain a lucrative strategy for some, while others might covertly siphon funds from charitable organizations, tapping into the goodwill of unsuspecting donors.

However, it is in the shadows of the global financial architecture where the real game intensifies. Hawala systems, an ancient trust-based money transfer mechanism, have been exploited due to their anonymity and lack of formal record-keeping. Parallelly, the digital revolution has thrown open another Pandora's box. Cryptocurrencies, with their decentralized nature and anonymity, have emerged as a potential haven for terrorist financing, offering layers of concealment that traditional banking cannot.

Furthermore, the fluidity of global trade and the vast expanse of the internet have enabled illicit online marketplaces, trafficking, and smuggling routes to become funding sources. From peddling counterfeit goods to illegal arms sales, the digital age has expanded the financial frontier for terrorist entities.

In essence, to truly grasp the magnitude and intricacies of terrorist operations, one must follow the money trail, recognizing its pivotal role in the life cycle of terrorist undertakings. It is a dynamic, evolving dance between global enforcement agencies and terrorist financiers, where each move precipitates a countermove, underscoring the relentless adaptability and innovation of these malevolent entities in their quest for resources.

Sources of Terrorist Funding: Illicit Activities, State Support, and Charitable Fronts

Terrorist organizations, while ideologically driven, function much like multifaceted corporations when it comes to their financing, tapping into both the underbelly and the facade of global commerce and philanthropy. Delving into the matrix of their financial sources, one is met with an intricate tapestry of converging revenue streams that sustain the gears of terror machinery.

The shadowy realms of illicit markets serve as the lifeblood for many extremist groups, providing them with the funds essential for their operations. A large slice of their financing is drawn from the depths of these underground economies. The drug trade, with its sprawling global networks, stands out as a major contributor. The opium fields of Afghanistan, the notorious golden triangle in Southeast Asia, and the formidable drug cartels of Latin America have, whether unintentionally or deliberately, channeled significant resources into the hands of terror outfits. Beyond the narcotics domain, an array of smuggling activities further pads these terror budgets. This includes not only the illicit trading of petroleum and precious antiquities but also the heart-wrenching industry of human trafficking and the clandestine trade of endangered wildlife. These underhanded endeavors, vast and deeply entrenched, create a formidable financial infrastructure supporting global terrorism.

Yet, the funding landscape is not just populated by the shadows of the criminal underworld. The political machinations of state-sponsored terrorism provide another layer of complexity. Some nation-states, driven by geopolitical ambitions, have been implicated in covertly channeling resources to terrorist groups. These proxy warriors, armed and bankrolled by their state benefactors, then act as extended arms of state policy, furthering national interests without direct accountability or overt warfare.

However, perhaps the most insidious and paradoxical of these funding mechanisms is the exploitation of charitable organizations. Under the veneer of philanthropy, certain charities have been manipulated or established as fronts for terror financing. Donors, often oblivious to the malevolent redirection of their contributions, believe they are aiding humanitarian causes, when in reality, their funds might be channeled into radicalization campaigns, arms procurement, or attack logistics. This exploitation of human compassion not only furnishes terrorists with financial support but also sows the seeds of mistrust in the philanthropic arena.

In navigating this multifaceted financial landscape, it becomes evident that terrorist financing is not a straightforward affair. It is a confluence of dark market trades, political intrigue, and subverted humanity. Understanding this multifarious funding matrix is crucial, not just for comprehending the operational longevity of terrorist groups but also for crafting strategies to staunch the flow of funds that give life to their violent endeavors.

Money Laundering and Hawala Systems

The financial machinery propelling terrorist organizations is not only complex in its sourcing but also intricate in its distribution and camouflage. Central to this obfuscation strategy is money laundering, a systematic process where illicitly acquired funds are funneled through a series of transactions designed to make the funds' origins murky, rendering them virtually 'clean' and difficult to trace. The complex nature of global finance provides ample avenues for these tainted funds to be mingled with legitimate assets, masking their nefarious origins. Real estate investments, shell corporations, and trading activities are among the myriad avenues exploited to give these funds an air of legitimacy.

Parallel to this world of intricate money laundering lies the ancient and predominantly trust-based hawala system. Originating in the medieval Islamic world, the hawala network operates on a simple principle of trust and balance. It bypasses the conventional banking infrastructure entirely. Instead, it relies on a network of brokers, or hawaladars, who facilitate the transfer of money based on mere trust and verbal codes, without any physical movement of funds. An individual wanting to send money provides the sum to a hawaladar, who then communicates with a counterpart in the recipient's location, ensuring the money's equivalent is handed over. Settlements between these brokers might occur at a later time and can take various forms, including cash, goods, or services. What makes hawala particularly appealing to illicit operators, including terrorists, is its rapidity, minimal paper trail, and deep penetration in regions with limited banking infrastructure.

Both these mechanisms—money laundering with its calculated complexity and the age-old hawala with its discreet simplicity—pose formidable challenges to counter-terrorism financiers. While one manipulates the very intricacies of the global financial system to hide in plain sight, the other eschews the system entirely, operating in the shadows of trust-based exchanges. Tackling these clandestine channels necessitates a combination of rigorous international financial oversight, grassroots intelligence operations, and an in-depth understanding of regional cultural and financial practices.

International Efforts to Disrupt Terrorist Financing

As terrorism morphed into a transnational menace, the need for a coordinated, global approach to throttle its financial pathways became starkly evident. Recognizing this, the international community, over the years, has increased its efforts, formulating strategies and building frameworks to disrupt the lifelines of terrorist funding. Foremost among these efforts are sanctions—both targeted and comprehensive—imposed by global powerhouses and international bodies such as the United States and United Nations. These sanctions not only single out individuals and entities associated with terrorist acts but also restrict their access to the global financial system, squeezing their resources.

Further cementing these efforts, asset freezing has emerged as a robust tool, placing an immediate stranglehold on identified funds linked to terrorist entities. This measure not only stalls ongoing operations but also serves as a deterrent for potential financiers wary of exposure and/or financial losses. Complementing these efforts are stringent regulatory frameworks established globally. For instance, the Financial Action Task Force (FATF) has been instrumental in setting global standards in combating terrorist financing. Through its evolving recommendations, countries are urged to bolster their financial systems, ensuring transparency, adherence to due diligence, and reporting of suspicious activities.

Another notable stride is the emphasis on cross-border intelligence sharing. Leveraging technological advancements, countries now share real-time data about dubious financial transactions, expediting the detection and investigation processes. This international camaraderie, characterized by shared databases and joint task forces, showcases a unified front against a common enemy.

Yet, as these measures tighten the noose around conventional channels, the battleground evolves, with terrorists continually seeking and often finding newer, more covert avenues for finance. The cat-and-mouse game continues, but what remains undiminished is the international community's resolve to starve terrorism of its financial lifeblood. Through a synthesis of regulations, technology, and international cooperation, the endeavor is not just to chase but to anticipate and thwart.

Case Studies of Successful Disruption and Challenges Ahead

In the constantly evolving landscape of terrorist financing, various instances stand as testimony to both the successes of international efforts and the adaptability of terrorist networks. The following case studies have aided in discerning patterns, strategies, and the path ahead.

The Al-Barakaat Network: In the wake of the catastrophic events of 9/11, the global spotlight turned to the intricate web of financial systems that might have facilitated terror funding. One particular entity that came under scrutiny was Al-Barakaat Network. Based in Somalia, this conglomerate operated both as a financial and telecommunications nexus. While it offered essential services to many within Somalia, international intelligence agencies grew increasingly suspicious that the network was channeling funds to Al-Qaeda.

This led to an unprecedented international collaboration, as countries across the globe, armed with actionable intelligence, moved swiftly to neutralize the perceived threat. Assets were frozen, and the expansive operations of Al-Barakaat were systematically shut down in a multitude of countries. This episode not only highlighted the crucial role of global cooperation in countering terrorism but also set a precedent for how to effectively dismantle the financial lifelines of extremist groups. The lesson gleaned from this endeavor was abundantly clear: when robust intelligence gathering is seamlessly integrated with swift, coordinated international responses, even the most entrenched financial networks supporting terrorism can be rendered impotent.

The Hezballah Funding via South American Drug Trade: The symbiotic relationship between global criminal enterprises and extremist group funding has become increasingly evident, illustrated starkly by the operations of Hezballah, the Lebanon-based militant faction. For numerous years, this group has found a foothold in the tri-border nexus of South America, where the territories of Argentina, Brazil, and Paraguay intertwine. This region, characterized by its intricate jurisdictions and notorious for a variety of underground activities, has emerged as a hotbed for the drug trade.

Pervasive investigations into these dealings have revealed an alarmingly complex network; South American drug lords, shadowy money launderers, and Hezballah's financial architects seem to be operating in a covert yet coordinated dance of illicit financial flows. In response to these discoveries, international agencies have embarked on a multi-pronged approach. Ground operations have been launched to dismantle the core drug trade infrastructure, while surgical financial strikes in the form of sanctions target those identified as the monetary middlemen for Hezballah. This entire scenario serves as a strong reminder: the world of terrorist financing often blurs lines with other criminal spheres, emphasizing the need for a far-reaching strategy in counter-terrorism efforts.

ISIS and Oil Revenues: As ISIS burgeoned into one of history's most formidable extremist entities, it astutely capitalized on the oil fields it had wrested control of, transforming them into veritable lifelines for its operations. These oil fields, scattered across the territories it dominated, became prolific sources of revenue, pouring significant funds into the group's coffers. The international community, recognizing the strategic importance of these resources to ISIS, devised a multi-tiered response. Targeted airstrikes meticulously zeroed in on the oil infrastructure, seeking to disrupt the extraction, refining, and transportation processes.

Concurrently, sanctions were imposed on individuals and entities implicated in the purchase and distribution of this illicit oil. These concerted efforts bore fruit, precipitating a sharp decline in the oil revenues that had once buoyed ISIS. The overarching lesson drawn from this episode underscores the efficacy of a focused strategy: by pinpointing and assailing primary revenue streams, it is possible to significantly impede, if not cripple, a terrorist organization's operational momentum and expansive capabilities.

Challenges Ahead: As we navigate the landscape of counter-terrorism financing, the successes achieved thus far certainly serve as beacons of progress, but they also illuminate the ever-evolving challenges that lie ahead. It is a game of adaptation: as the noose tightens around traditional financial arteries that terrorists have depended upon, these nefarious actors nimbly shift to uncharted terrains. Cryptocurrencies, for instance, have emerged as an attractive alternative for them. With their core attributes of anonymity and decentralization, these digital currencies offer an obfuscating shield against detection, allowing illicit transactions to glide beneath the conventional radar.

Moreover, there is a discernible trend away from monolithic financing structures towards more dispersed strategies. As traditional fundraising avenues are systematically clamped down upon, extremist groups demonstrate their adaptability, harnessing the potential of the digital age. They are increasingly soliciting micro-financing, ingeniously tapping into online platforms and exploiting crowd-funding methodologies. These innovative tactics, decentralized and often masked under benign facades, pose new quandaries for those committed to choking off the financial lifelines of terrorist organizations. The road ahead, it seems, requires constant vigilance and adaptability in the face of shifting terrorist financing paradigms.

Chapter 14:
Terrorism's Impact on Society - Fear, Policy, and Adaptation

Terrorist acts, stark in their violence and unpredictability, do more than just cause immediate destruction and loss of life. They are, in essence, dark symphonies meticulously orchestrated to resonate far beyond the immediate locus of devastation. Through the smoke and debris, the true intent emerges: to seed fear, disrupt normalcy, and manipulate the collective psyche of societies.

Each act of terrorism, however isolated it might seem, carries with it a profound narrative. These violent episodes aim to challenge the very notions of security and safety, making every individual feel vulnerable even within the sanctuaries of their homes or communities. By targeting symbols of cultural, economic, or political significance, terrorists strive to send a message that no place is truly safe, no institution untouchable.

Furthermore, the shockwaves triggered by such acts are intended to ripple through the corridors of power, influencing policy decisions. Governments, under immense public pressure in the aftermath of attacks, might make hasty decisions, be it deploying troops, altering foreign policy, or enacting strict security measures. Such reactions, often knee-jerk and emotionally charged, can sometimes play into the hands of extremist factions, furthering their agendas.

But perhaps the most insidious impact of terrorism lies in its ability to subtly alter the fabric of communities. Trust, once a given, becomes a luxury. Neighbor might view neighbor with suspicion, and divides — be they ethnic, religious, or political — can deepen. Communities that once celebrated diversity might find themselves fragmenting, with walls of mistrust rising between different groups.

Living in the Shadow of Fear

In the wake of a terrorist attack, the immediate, tangible destruction often captures global attention—crumbling buildings, killed and injured, and streets marked by chaos. However, lurking beneath this overt devastation is a more insidious and pervasive aftermath: the profound psychological impact on the human psyche. Regardless of direct exposure, the specter of terrorism can induce deep-seated traumas, forever altering one's perception of safety and normalcy.

For those who witness these heinous acts firsthand, the memories can be haunting. The cacophony of sirens, the smell of smoke, and the visceral fear of the unknown can etch permanent marks on their minds. Such traumatic experiences can manifest in a range of disorders, from post-traumatic stress disorder (PTSD) to acute stress reactions. Sleep disturbances, flashbacks, and heightened vigilance become unwelcome staples of their daily lives.

Yet, the ripples of these events extend far beyond the immediate vicinity of the attacks. Thanks to the ever-present media, images and narratives of these horrors are broadcasted into living rooms around the world. For many, the relentless coverage can induce a state of perpetual anxiety, leading to a phenomenon known as vicarious traumatization. This sense of second-hand trauma can be just as debilitating, cultivating a pervasive fear of public spaces, distrust of strangers, and a general sense of impending doom.

Furthermore, the collective psyche of entire communities or nations can be shifted. Societal behaviors transform—people might avoid crowded places, change daily routines, or become overly protective of loved ones. The social fabric can undergo subtle changes, with increased suspicion, reduced communal activities, and a heightened sense of 'us versus them.'

The psychological toll of terrorism is a silent epidemic, affecting vast swaths of populations in a myriad of ways. While the physical damages might be repaired and wounds may heal, the invisible scars on the collective conscience require a different kind of healing—one that entails empathy, understanding, and concerted efforts to rebuild a sense of safety and unity.

In an era where the shadow of terrorism looms large, the effects of this menace are not just relegated to the immediate aftermath of an attack. Instead, it subtly permeates the ordinary, altering the very rhythms and routines that define daily life. The undercurrent of unease, sometimes overt and sometimes latent, influences decisions, both major and minute, which were once taken without a second thought.

Public events, which were once symbols of communal togetherness and celebration, might now be viewed through a lens of apprehension. The excitement of attending a crowded concert, participating in a festival, or even just watching a fireworks display on New Year's Eve can be overshadowed by the nagging question: "Is it safe?" This hesitancy can lead to reduced attendance, dampening the very spirit of such events.

Similarly, the once-simple joys of traveling have acquired a new layer of complexity. Families planning vacations may find themselves weighing the beauty and appeal of a destination against its perceived safety. Historical landmarks, bustling markets, and iconic festivals, which might have been top attractions, could now be approached with caution or even avoided altogether. The tourism industry, in turn, feels the pinch, as once-thriving destinations see dwindling numbers.

Even daily commutes are not immune. Individuals might alter their routes to avoid busy transit hubs or prefer less crowded times, adding extra hours to their week just to sidestep potential hotspots. The spontaneous spirit of urban life—grabbing a coffee at a popular cafe, spontaneously meeting friends at a city square, or taking a late-night walk—can be tempered by an ever-present sense of vigilance.

In summation, the sinister impact of terrorism extends its reach into the mundane, transforming the tapestry of daily life into one punctuated by caution and second-guessing. While resilience remains a defining human trait, the challenge lies in reclaiming the spontaneity and joy of life amidst the specter of threat.

Policy Reactions and Shifts

The rise of global terrorism has necessitated a seismic shift in policymaking, compelling governments worldwide to reevaluate their internal and external security protocols. In an endeavor to fortify their nations against these threats, many have chosen the legislative path, crafting laws that they believe will protect citizens while curbing the growth of extremist ideologies.

One of the most pronounced examples of this legislative reaction in the United States is the USA PATRIOT Act. Enacted swiftly after the tragic events of September 11, 2001, this act expanded the federal government's surveillance and investigatory powers, aiming to preemptively identify and neutralize threats. While its provisions, such as eased restrictions for wiretapping and broader financial scrutiny, were hailed by many as essential tools for a new age of security, they also ignited debates on personal freedoms and the potential for governmental overreach.

Across the Atlantic, the U.K. grappled with its share of terrorist threats, leading to the enactment of the Prevention of Terrorism Act. This legislation granted the government powers to impose control orders on individuals suspected of involvement in terrorist activities, even if they had not been formally charged or tried. While its objective was clear—to mitigate potential threats before they could materialize—it too spurred controversies, particularly regarding civil liberties and the due process of law.

These legislative endeavors underscore a broader global trend: the delicate, often contentious, balancing act between national security and individual rights. While the urgency to protect is palpable and genuine, the challenge lies in ensuring that these policy responses do not inadvertently erode the very freedoms and values they seek to defend. As societies navigate this complex terrain, the dialogue surrounding these laws becomes not just about security but also about the essence of democracy, the sanctity of individual rights, and the vision of the kind of world we wish to reside in.

The tumultuous interplay between terrorism and state responses has, in many instances, cast a shadow over the broader discourse of migration and border control. When a terrorist act is traced back to individuals with foreign connections or origins, the ripple effect often culminates in heightened border scrutiny and revisited immigration policies, as nations grapple with the task of ensuring security while upholding values of openness and human rights.

In the aftermath of such attacks, border checkpoints might become more militarized, with an increase in guards, more thorough inspections, and advanced technology deployments, such as biometric scanning and facial recognition systems. These measures aim to detect and deter potential threats, making it harder for malign actors to enter and operate within a country.

Yet, within the realm of immigration policy is where the ramifications are perhaps most profound. The public's fear, often fueled by sensationalist media coverage and political rhetoric, can push governments toward implementing more restrictive visa regimes, reducing refugee intake, or even enacting travel bans against certain nationalities. These decisions, while sometimes popular in the short term, have deeper, long-term implications. They can strain diplomatic ties, stymie cultural exchange, and, critically, paint entire communities with a broad brush, leading to a perception that equates migration with threat.

Moreover, these policies can inadvertently exacerbate the refugee crises worldwide. As nations shutter their doors, thousands fleeing genuine threats—be it from war, persecution, or poverty—are left in limbo, often in overcrowded camps or dangerous transit routes as seen during the rise of ISIS.

In essence, while the instinct to fortify borders in the face of perceived external threats is understandable, it necessitates a nuanced approach. The challenge for global leaders is to strike a balance: ensuring the safety of their citizens without compromising the inherent values of openness, human rights, and international cooperation that have been hallmarks of a connected world.

Economic Repercussions

In the wake of a terrorist attack, the immediate focus often gravitates towards the heart-wrenching loss of lives and the indelible emotional scars imprinted on communities. Yet, beyond this immediate sorrow exists a more insidious and sometimes overlooked aftermath: the profound economic ramifications that ripple out, subtly yet significantly shaping the trajectory of affected societies.

In the direct aftermath of an attack, infrastructure — be it transportation hubs, commercial centers, or utilities — may suffer extensive damage, necessitating costly repairs and sometimes even full-scale reconstructions. This immediate destruction can disrupt the normal ebb and flow of commerce and transportation, leading to short-term economic slowdowns or stagnation.

Businesses, especially those in close proximity to the attack or those directly targeted, face immediate challenges. Apart from physical damages, there can be interruptions in their supply chains, loss of customers, and sometimes, a need to compensate affected employees or families. Small businesses, in particular, may find it challenging to recover without substantial financial aid.

Furthermore, the overarching market is not immune to the impact of such events. Stock markets often react adversely to terrorist incidents, with indices plunging due to investor uncertainty and a temporary loss of confidence. Sectors particularly sensitive to perceptions of safety, such as tourism and aviation, can experience more prolonged downturns. Tourist hotspots might witness a decline in visitors, leading to reduced income for local businesses and potentially impacting employment in the region.

While the emotional and social impacts of terrorism are undeniably profound, the economic aftermath is a testament to the comprehensive nature of the challenges that societies face post-attack. Addressing these economic challenges requires not only immediate relief measures but also a long-term strategy to restore investor confidence, support affected businesses, and ensure the resilience of the economic ecosystem in the face of future threats.

An additional evident repercussion surfaces in the sectors of tourism and foreign investment. For places that were once vibrant hubs for travelers, terrorist incidents can swiftly tarnish their allure, painting them as high-risk zones or 'hot spots,' Tourists, driven by safety concerns and often influenced by travel advisories, might opt for perceived 'safer' destinations, leading to a sharp decline in visitor numbers. This has cascading effects on the local economy: hotels witness reduced occupancy, restaurants grapple with fewer patrons, and local artisans and vendors face dwindling sales.

Beyond the tangible loss in tourism revenue, the region's global image as a viable investment destination also takes a hit. Foreign investors, always wary of unpredictability and instability, might hesitate to invest in areas perceived as terrorism-prone. Whether it is establishing new businesses, expanding existing ones, or even entering into trade agreements, the specter of terrorism introduces an element of risk that many investors are unwilling to shoulder. This reluctance to invest not only hampers immediate economic growth but can also stifle long-term developmental prospects, potentially leading to reduced job creation and a constrained economic landscape.

The repercussions of these declines in tourism and investment are profound. They compound the challenges faced by regions already grappling with the immediate aftermath of terrorism, making recovery a daunting task. It underscores the necessity for improved counter-terrorism strategies that not only address security concerns but also focus on rebuilding and promoting the regional image, ensuring that the economic heartbeat of the affected areas can be revived and sustained in the long term.

One of the more insidious effects manifests in the ballooning budgets allocated to counter-terrorism. Nations, especially those that have faced the brunt of terror attacks or perceive themselves as prime targets, often find themselves channeling vast financial resources into bolstering their security apparatus. This could mean heightened border controls, advanced surveillance systems, specialized training for law enforcement, or even the establishment of dedicated anti-terrorism units.

While such investments are undoubtedly crucial in the bid to ensure the safety of citizens and maintain internal stability, they come with their own set of challenges. This increase in security expenditure often necessitates the diversion of funds from other essential areas such as healthcare, education, infrastructure, and social welfare. The ramifications of this can be long-term: a generation might receive a lesser quality of education, critical health interventions could be delayed, and infrastructure projects, vital for economic growth, might be shelved.

Furthermore, this reallocation of budget priorities can sometimes lead to societal discontent, especially if citizens feel that their immediate needs are being sidelined in favor of security measures that, while important, might seem distant or abstract to their daily lives. This delicate balancing act — ensuring robust security without compromising on other developmental needs — is a challenge that many governments grapple within the modern era.

Societal Cohesion and Fragmentation

One of the most heartening phenomena to witness post an attack is the remarkable solidarity shown by communities. In the aftermath of profound tragedies like 9/11 in the U.S. or the Charlie Hebdo shooting in France, the global community responded not with fragmentation, but with an overwhelming sense of cohesion. Streets filled with candlelight vigils, monuments worldwide were lit in national colors of the affected country, and social media platforms brimmed with messages of solidarity, support, and resilience. Such gestures go beyond mere expressions of sympathy; they symbolize a collective stand against the forces of hatred, a reaffirmation of shared values, and the undying spirit of humanity in the face of adversity.

However, this unity is just one side of the coin. These very events can also expose underlying societal fissures, sometimes leading to misplaced blame, scapegoating, and an increase in divisive rhetoric. Vulnerable groups, especially if they share a superficial association with the perpetrators (like religion or ethnicity), might face unwarranted suspicion, discrimination, or even violence. Thus, while the immediate aftermath might showcase commendable unity, the subsequent weeks and months can reveal underlying tensions, which if unchecked, can lead to societal fragmentation.

In essence, the aftermath of terrorism presents a dichotomy. On one hand, it reveals the inherent strength of communities, their capacity to come together, heal, and rebuild. On the other hand, it can act as a litmus test for societal cohesion, revealing the latent prejudices and biases that might exist just beneath the surface. It is a reminder that while solidarity in adversity is commendable, ensuring lasting cohesion requires continuous dialogue, understanding, and efforts towards belonging.

Furthermore, a society's response to a terrorist attack can often teeter between cohesion and division. When acts of terror are attributed, rightly or wrongly, to particular ethnic or religious groups, the ripple effect can be profoundly destabilizing. Even though the perpetrators might represent a minuscule fringe with beliefs far removed from the broader community they are associated with, generalizations can rapidly set in. This can lead to sweeping suspicions, where entire communities become unjustly painted with the same brush of extremism.

The manifestations of this mistrust can range from subtle changes in interpersonal dynamics to more overt and damaging actions. It is not uncommon to witness a surge in discriminatory behavior, whether in the form of racial profiling, workplace discrimination, or social ostracization. In more extreme cases, this suspicion can escalate into outright hostility, resulting in hate crimes, verbal abuse, and even physical violence against members of the denigrated community. These actions not only inflict harm upon innocent individuals but also erode the very fabric of societal harmony.

This descent into mistrust is particularly tragic given that the targeted communities often share in the grief and condemnation of the terrorist act. By becoming victims of prejudice, they face a dual trauma: the pain of the attack itself and the subsequent burden of unwarranted suspicion. For societies aiming for harmony and peace, it is crucial to recognize and resist these divisive tendencies. Genuine understanding, robust community outreach, and continuous education are pivotal in ensuring that the bonds of trust, once frayed, can be mended and fortified against future strains.

How Terrorism Morphs Culture and Art

The ever-evolving tapestry of culture and art holds within its intricate patterns the chronicles of human experience. From the dawn of human civilization, this tapestry has woven tales of our triumphs, failures, fears, and aspirations. Consider the literary masterpieces that grace our libraries: they are not mere collections of words, but reservoirs of emotions, thoughts, and reflections of the epochs they were birthed in. Likewise, the visual arts—paintings, sculptures, and installations—serve as silent yet powerful witnesses to the zeitgeist of their respective eras.

Yet, in more contemporary settings, as the world grapples with the complex and often devastating ramifications of terrorism, the role of art and culture becomes even more pertinent. What is it about terrorism that prompts such profound introspection within the artistic community? The reason lies in its profound disruption of the human narrative. It shatters the semblance of normalcy, rips apart the fabric of everyday life, and confronts us with our own vulnerabilities.

Artists, whether wielding a pen, a brush, or a camera, have never been mere bystanders in this unfolding drama. Take, for instance, a novel. Within its pages, an author might compare the serenity of everyday life against the abrupt chaos of a terrorist act, weaving a narrative that alternates between despair and hope, between the mundane and the catastrophic. Similarly, in the world of cinema, filmmakers often encapsulate the harrowing aftermath of terror, sometimes focusing on the macroscopic societal impacts, and at other times, narrowing in on the microscopic, personal agonies.

Yet, amidst the cacophony of chaos and the looming shadows of dread, there emerges a consistent thread in the narrative of art—a testament to human resilience. Short verses of poetry might capture fleeting moments of despair, while sprawling epics lay out grandiose visions of a society reborn from its ashes. Paintings may shift between dark, brooding colors representing desolation and vibrant hues symbolizing hope.

Art emerges as a powerful humanitarian response, addressing the challenges posed by terrorism with resilience and defiance. While it unflinchingly portrays the depth of societal anxieties, it equally champions the indomitable human spirit that refuses to be cowed. Through varied sentence lengths, diverse mediums, and myriad perspectives, the world of art and culture continuously engages in a dialogue with society, reminding us that even in the face of overwhelming darkness, the human spirit, like art, perseveres and evolves.

The aftershocks of terrorist acts do not merely end with the immediate damage; they reverberate through the annals of time, shaping societies, politics, and human relationships. It is a daunting ripple, one that disturbs the waters of collective memory, leaving an indelible mark. But as we have seen, within this maelstrom emerges a beacon of hope. Societies, in their enduring spirit, have continuously risen from the ashes, choosing remembrance over oblivion.

Memorials become the embodiment of this choice. They are not just sites to mourn the lost but also arenas to celebrate humanity's unwavering spirit. Each candle lit, each flower laid, and each tear shed at these places brings to the forefront the power of collective memory and the shared resolve to move forward, even as we never forget. Through these acts of remembrance, communities not only memorialize the past but also pave the way for a future fortified against such atrocities, ensuring that the sacrifices of many are etched in the annals of time, serving as both a warning and an inspiration for generations to come.

Chapter 15:
The Global Response - Role of International Organizations in Combating Terrorism

As the strands of terrorism continue to spread an intricate web across nations, the imperative for a unified global response has never been more critical. International organizations, be it the United Nations, NATO, or Interpol, play a pivotal role in this matrix. These institutions serve not only as a platform for dialogue but as crucibles where strategies are forged, shared, and refined. With their ability to bring together diverse nations under a singular umbrella, they champion the ethos of collective security. Beyond mere partnerships, these organizations pool intelligence, technologies, and best practices, ensuring that nations, both big and small, are armed with the knowledge and tools needed to counter threats.

By fostering a climate of trust and cooperation, international organizations help transcend political divides, thereby strengthening global resilience against the comprehensive challenges of terrorism. The shared databases, training programs, and humanitarian initiatives they champion are testament to the belief that in unity lies the best defense against the disruptive forces of extremism. Through their concerted efforts, the message rings clear: terrorism, no matter where it manifests, is a shared adversary that demands a collective, well-coordinated response.

The Unites States Counter-Terrorism Programs

Following the devastating terrorist attacks on September 11, 2001, the United States rapidly introduced a series of programs and measures to fortify national security and deter potential terrorist threats. The USA PATRIOT Act of 2001 was one such initiative that significantly augmented the government's ability to survey and investigate, raising civil liberties concerns for many. In 2002, the Department of Homeland Security (DHS) was established, amalgamating 22 distinct federal entities into a single cohesive unit, primarily tasked with combatting domestic emergencies, especially terrorism. Concurrently, the Transportation Security Administration (TSA) was formed, focusing on enhancing security across U.S. transport systems, notably intensifying airport security protocols.

By 2004, the National Counter-terrorism Center (NCTC) was inaugurated, becoming the principal body for assimilating and analyzing intelligence on terrorism. Subsequent years witnessed several modifications to the Foreign Intelligence Surveillance Act (FISA) to address contemporary communication paradigms, thereby broadening governmental surveillance purview. Controversially, in the aftermath of the attacks, the CIA adopted Enhanced Interrogation Techniques, later widely condemned as torture, leading to the program's discontinuation in 2009.

The Real ID Act of 2005 tightened regulations surrounding driver's license issuance, and the Terrorist Finance Tracking Program (TFTP) was initiated to monitor the financial activities of suspected terrorists. The 2012 National Defense Authorization Act (NDAA) incorporated disputed clauses pertaining to the indeterminate detention of terror suspects, even if they were U.S. citizens. Recognizing the need for a consolidated effort, the Information Sharing Environment (ISE) was created, promoting inter-agency collaboration on terrorism-related information.

Additionally, the National Security Entry-Exit Registration System (NSEERS) (2002-2011) mandated periodic registration for specific non-citizens in the U.S., though it was later criticized for predominantly targeting Muslims. These endeavors form part of the extensive U.S. post-9/11 counter-terrorism strategy, often inciting discussions about the equilibrium between ensuring national security and preserving civil liberties.

The United Nations and Its Counter-terrorism Initiatives

One of the most significant reactions of 9/11 was the establishment of the UN Counter-terrorism Committee (CTC). Recognizing that terrorism was not just an isolated threat to one nation, but a global menace that transcended borders, cultures, and ideologies, the international community rallied to put forth a collective front against this shared adversary. The CTC's inception highlighted this newfound global urgency. Formulated under the aegis of the United Nations, the Committee aimed to stymie the proliferation of terrorist activities and bolster the capacity of member states to combat terroristic threats. By facilitating enhanced cooperation, information exchange, and synchronization of efforts, the CTC emerged as a beacon of collective resilience and determination in a world shaken to its core.

Designed as a bulwark against the malevolent spread of extremist ideologies and actions, the CTC's primary mandate revolves around augmenting the defenses of UN member states. Its diverse objectives cover the spectrum of counter-terrorism measures. Recognizing that terrorists often exploit porous borders, the committee has been unrelenting in its advocacy for stringent border controls, ensuring that terrorists cannot find safe havens or move unencumbered. But the CTC's mission did not stop at prevention. It went on the offensive, underlining the imperative of a robust criminal justice system that can prosecute and penalize those involved in these heinous acts. Moreover, in today's globalized world where money flows seamlessly across borders, the CTC's emphasis on countering the financing of terrorism is of paramount importance. By targeting their financial networks and resources, the CTC's aim is to cripple these organizations from within.

While the establishment of the CTC marked a significant stride against the war on terrorism, it soon became evident that the multi-layered nature of terrorism required an even more comprehensive framework. This realization culminated in the formation of the UN Office of Counter-Terrorism (UNOCT). Entrusted with a mission both vast and pivotal, the UNOCT functions as the central hub for coordinating all counter-terrorism endeavors within the United Nations' expansive system. Its primary aim is to ensure a synchronized strategy, optimize resource allocation, and maximize collective efforts. Acting as a bridge, the UNOCT facilitates seamless collaboration, drawing upon the specialized expertise and insights from various UN member states.

Beyond its role as a coordinating entity, the UNOCT is deeply engaged in fortifying nations through capacity-building programs. Grasping the reality that the global counter-terrorism network is only as resilient as its most vulnerable member, the office concentrates on empowering every UN member with the requisite knowledge, tools, and resources to confront the evolving menace of terrorism. At the heart of the UNOCT's endeavors is a resounding affirmation of a foundational belief: the collective strength, wisdom, and determination of the global community remain the most formidable deterrent against the looming specter of terrorism.

The Role of NATO

The North Atlantic Treaty Organization (NATO), originally conceived in the backdrop of Cold War geopolitics, has over time recalibrated its mission in response to the evolving nature of global threats. Central to its ethos is Article 5, a testament to the alliance's unyielding commitment to mutual defense. Its declaration that an attack on one member is tantamount to an attack on all encapsulates the essence of collective defense. While this provision remained dormant for much of NATO's history, the cataclysmic events of 9/11 triggered its first-ever invocation. By doing so, NATO not only exhibited its unwavering support for the United States but also sent a resounding message: terrorism, in all its forms, was a shared adversary.

But NATO's counter-terrorism initiatives go beyond mere posturing. Recognizing that foreknowledge is pivotal in preempting threats, the alliance places an immense emphasis on intelligence sharing. By creating platforms and protocols for member states to pool their intel, NATO ensures that vital information concerning potential threats does not get misplaced. This collaborative approach multiplies the eyes and ears on potential threats, enhancing the chances of early detection and neutralization. Furthermore, NATO's involvement in joint operations, as witnessed in Afghanistan and Iraq, exemplifies its commitment to not just defense but active confrontation of terrorist entities. Such operations not only aim to dismantle the immediate threat but also to address root causes by stabilizing regions and reducing the vacuum in which extremism thrives.

NATO's approach to terrorism underscores a key realization: In unity and collective action lie the most formidable deterrents to those who seek to fracture peace and global stability.

Financial Countermeasures: The FATF

The Financial Action Task Force (FATF) stands as a bulwark against the sophisticated financial networks that underpin terrorist operations and illicit activities worldwide. As an inter-governmental organization, the FATF's mandate transcends merely identifying and remedying vulnerabilities in financial systems. Its core mission lies in obstructing the lifeblood of terrorism: finance. By formulating and promoting robust international standards, the FATF ensures that financial systems globally are resistant to abuse by illicit entities. But the task force does not stop at merely setting these benchmarks. A rigorous evaluation mechanism assesses member countries on their adherence to these standards.

Such evaluations are instrumental in not only identifying potential chinks in the armor but also in exerting diplomatic pressure on nations to fortify their financial defenses. Through these measures, the FATF seeks to choke off the financial channels that could otherwise be exploited to fund acts of terror. The significance of this organization's work cannot be understated, for in its endeavors lies the realization that while ideology drives extremists, it is funds that enable their operations. By stemming the flow of money, the FATF is essentially squeezing the operational capacity of terrorist entities, ensuring that their malevolent intentions remain unfulfilled.

Regional Efforts

The nature of terrorism, influenced by diverse historical, socio-economic, and geopolitical factors, necessitates an equally nuanced response, particularly at the regional level where countries often grapple with shared challenges. Several regional blocs, appreciating the interconnected dynamics at play, have tailored their counter-terrorism strategies to address the unique challenges and opportunities within their specific contexts.

In the heart of Southeast Asia, the Association of Southeast Asian Nations (ASEAN) offers an intriguing study in collaborative counter-terrorism. Recognizing the intricate web of shared borders, trade routes, cultural ties, and, in some instances, shared security threats, ASEAN has adopted a robust counter-terrorism strategy. Central to this approach is the emphasis on intelligence-sharing. With terrorism's transnational nature, information becomes a currency of immense value, and pooling resources in this domain ensures that member states can preempt and respond to threats more effectively. Unified law enforcement training and protocols ensure that the bloc presents a united front, negating potential loopholes that might be exploited by malicious entities. Furthermore, given the fluidity of movement within the region, strengthened border controls act as vital checkpoints to monitor and prevent the transit of potential terrorists.

Meanwhile, the European continent presents its own set of challenges and solutions. The European Union (EU), a testament to post-war European solidarity and integration, has evolved a distinctive counter-terrorism model. While the urgency of addressing immediate threats remains paramount, the EU has chosen to invest equally in addressing the root causes of radicalization. This is manifested through the role of the Counter-terrorism Coordinator, a pivotal figure who liaises across member states to ensure a harmonized approach to threats.

The EU's strategy delves deep into the socio-political fabric of its member nations, promoting inclusive policies that foster social integration. By attempting to ensure that even the most marginalized communities find representation and voice, the EU hopes to stymie the feelings of alienation that often act as a precursor to radicalization. Furthermore, the emphasis on education is strategic; by introducing narratives of unity, tolerance, and coexistence in early education, the EU aims to counter extremist ideologies at their inception. For those who have, unfortunately, veered towards extremist ideologies, deradicalization programs offer a beacon of hope, ensuring that they are not lost but are instead offered pathways back to integration and societal contribution.

In essence, both ASEAN and the EU, despite their distinct geopolitical contexts, underscore a relevant truth in their counter-terrorism approaches: that cooperation, mutual understanding, and a judicious blend of immediate action and long-term strategy are pivotal in the global fight against terrorism.

Challenges and Critiques

In the global fight against terrorism, international cooperation is deemed indispensable. The transnational nature of terrorism, characterized by its ability to leapfrog borders and exploit international chasms, demands a unified, collective response. However, this global collaborative paradigm is not devoid of challenges.

Foremost among these is the delicate balance between collective action and the principle of national sovereignty. Nations, built upon the bedrock of self-determination and governance autonomy, are often protective of their sovereign rights. While they may acknowledge the necessity of international collaboration in counter-terrorism, the interventions of global bodies, especially when they appear to override national decisions or encroach upon domestic policies, can be viewed as unwarranted external intrusions. Such perceptions can be further magnified if the international bodies' decisions seem to be driven by the dominant political or economic interests of a few member states rather than a genuine collective will.

Coupled with this is the complicated challenge of coordination and bureaucracy. International counter-terrorism involves a mixture of entities — regional blocs, global organizations, specialized agencies, and coalitions — each with its own mandate, operational mode, and decision-making apparatus. The sheer number of stakeholders and the complexity of their interactions can inadvertently lead to overlaps, gaps, and inefficiencies. For instance, an intelligence report might get trapped in the vortex of bureaucratic procedures, delaying its relay to a nation that could act upon it. Or two agencies might find themselves working at cross-purposes, diluting the efficacy of their collective effort.

While the ethos of international cooperation in counter-terrorism is laudable and necessary, its practical implementation is fraught with challenges. The path forward necessitates a delicate dance — respecting the sanctity of national sovereignty while fostering a genuine collaborative spirit, and streamlining processes to ensure that the machinery of global cooperation is agile, responsive, and effective.

In an era where the lines between domestic and international are increasingly blurred, the role of international organizations in countering terrorism remains crucial. Their collective might, when harnessed effectively, can serve as a formidable barrier against the spread and impact of terrorist ideologies and actions.

Chapter 16:
The Role of Artificial Intelligence in Counter-Terrorism

In an era of ever-changing global security threats, the importance of leveraging advanced technology to bolster counter-terrorism measures has reached an unprecedented level of urgency. As we grapple with a wide range of challenges—from localized acts of violence to complex international terrorism networks—the limitations of traditional intelligence and security tactics become increasingly apparent. Against this backdrop, the emergence and integration of Artificial Intelligence (AI) into counter-terrorism frameworks offer not merely incremental improvements but transformative potential. AI is not just another tool in the toolkit; it is, in many respects, a game-changer.

Let us delve into a comprehensive exploration of the contributions of AI to counter-terrorism efforts. From the automated gathering and analysis of intelligence data to the coordinated management of crisis response, AI technologies present a suite of applications that redefine how we approach national and global security. But these advancements not only improve upon older processes; they fundamentally alter the nature of what is possible in counter-terrorism operations. For example, AI's ability to sift through enormous data sets enables a level of predictive analytics previously unattainable, allowing for pre-emptive actions that can thwart terror attacks before they come to fruition.

However, the integration of AI into sensitive domains like counter-terrorism also raises a host of ethical and practical challenges. Questions about data privacy, algorithmic bias, and the potential misuse of AI technologies cannot be overlooked. We must confront these challenges head-on, as failure to navigate them carefully could undermine public trust and even risk creating new avenues for abuse or error.

Data Analytics and Intelligence Gathering

When it comes to counter-terrorism, AI has emerged as a juggernaut, particularly for its ability to conduct data analytics. Unlike traditional methods of intelligence gathering, which are often sluggish and confined by human limitations, AI can move through vast oceans of data at a speed that defies comprehension. Why does this matter? Because speed is of the essence when lives are on the line.

For instance, consider a seemingly harmless social media update, one tiny blip in a sea of billions, that includes a particular keyword of interest. Would it catch a human analyst's eye? Possibly. But AI would undoubtedly flag it. And it does not stop there; AI also picks up on unusual financial activities, enigmatic communication patterns, and other digital breadcrumbs that might otherwise go unnoticed. By identifying these anomalies, which could potentially be warning signs of an impending threat, AI significantly boosts our capacity to foresee and avert acts of terrorism.

The advantages of AI are not just about speed and scale. It is also about timing, the pivotal element in any counter-terrorism strategy. AI does not just identify threats; it helps us act swiftly upon them. This technology narrows the often perilous time gap between spotting a potential threat and marshaling an effective response. When seconds count, the rapid dissemination of actionable intelligence can be the difference between tragedy and a crisis averted.

In the grand scale of modern counter-terrorism efforts, AI's role is not merely ancillary. It is transformative, revolutionizing the way we gather intelligence and, in the process, enhancing our collective security.

Natural Language Processing (NLP)

Navigating the murky waters of online extremism is a Herculean task that intelligence agencies continuously reckon with. Amidst this dark expanse of digital malevolence, AI serves as an illuminating lighthouse, courtesy of its cutting-edge Natural Language Processing (NLP) capabilities. AI not only skims the surface of online chatter but delves deep, sifting through text and audio across a myriad of languages, all in real-time.

However, NLP does far more than mere translation or rudimentary analysis. It pulls out thematic threads from the multiple corridors of online forums, social media, and hidden chat rooms. In layman's terms? It identifies what the bad guys are really talking about, unveiling references and coded language often employed by extremist factions. Another plus is the NLP's ability to summarize; it distills large volumes of content into bite-sized, actionable insights, allowing security agencies to be more agile in their responses.

But perhaps the most alluring feature of NLP is its proficiency in sentiment analysis. With this, it is not just about the 'what' but the 'how.' This technology has the ability to gauge the emotional temperature of a conversation, allowing a nuanced glimpse into the psychology and, therefore, the strategies at play within extremist circles. This sentiment analysis acts as a window, albeit a virtual one, into the minds behind propaganda campaigns and recruitment drives.

NLP is not just an ordinary tool it is a potent asset, a scalpel in the complex surgery of intelligence operations against online extremism. By dissecting text and audio, uncovering themes, summarizing vast tracts of data, and even identifying emotional undercurrents, it provides an unparalleled depth of understanding. And in a world where comprehension is the first step to counteraction, NPL is nothing short of revolutionary.

Facial Recognition Technologies

Traditionally, bustling public venues such as airports and train stations have been vulnerable hotspots for terrorist activities, posing intricate problems for security agencies. The introduction of AI-powered facial recognition technology has fundamentally altered the security landscape at these busy locales. No longer are we solely dependent on the vigilant gaze of human security staff. Instead, we now have at our disposal algorithms capable of analyzing countless faces in a matter of seconds. This is more than just technological progress; it is a seismic shift in how we approach public safety.

Imagine a bustling airport terminal, awash with a myriad of faces. Unbeknownst to the throng, an AI mechanism quietly performs scans, cross-referencing each facial imprint with a comprehensive database populated by known terrorists and watch-listed individuals. This is more than mere observation; it is nuanced recognition, capturing facial details with a level of precision unattainable by human scrutiny. And all of this occurs instantaneously, effectively eliminating the delays commonly associated with conventional security protocols.

What is truly revolutionary is the immediacy of the response this technology can trigger. The moment a match is found, alerts can be sent instantaneously to relevant security agencies or personnel on the ground. This rapid reaction time is invaluable, potentially disrupting plans for an imminent attack.

While the vulnerabilities of public spaces cannot be entirely eliminated, AI facial recognition technologies are closing the gap considerably. They offer a proactive approach to security, acting as both a deterrent and a rapid-response mechanism. In an era where threats constantly evolve, staying one step ahead is not just an advantage; it is a necessity.

Predictive Analytics

Staying one step ahead is more than a tactical advantage—it is often a matter of life and death. This is where predictive analytics, powered by machine learning algorithms, comes into play. Unlike reactive strategies that kick in post-incident, predictive analytics brings a decidedly pro-active edge to counter-terrorism efforts.

Archived secure databases are filled to the brim with historical data on acts of terror. While many might regard this as a static archive of bygone events, machine learning algorithms interpret it as a predictive manual for what lies ahead. Through detailed analysis of this wealth of information, AI assists security professionals in constructing comprehensive models. These models do more than just identify probable targets; they also predict the timing and tactics of impending attacks. This can be viewed as a form of advanced data alchemy, transforming raw numbers and facts into actionable insights for preemptive measures.

Naturally, predictive models have their limitations. They function within specific error margins, and their effectiveness is largely contingent upon the caliber of historical data they are trained on. However, even with these constraints, the intelligence they provide is undeniably crucial. Picture the ability to take proactive steps informed by plausible scenarios. Defensive structures could be bolstered around anticipated focal points of attack; monitoring systems could be heightened during periods recognized as high-risk; and security forces could be strategically positioned to counter specific attack modalities.

Even though predictive analytics does not offer a foolproof shield against terrorism, it significantly tilts the odds in favor of security agencies. By leveraging machine learning to foresee likely threats, we are not just reacting to terrorism—we are preempting it. And in a world where threats are increasingly sophisticated, this technology becomes not just an asset but a cornerstone in a layered defense strategy.

Surveillance and Reconnaissance

The integration of AI into surveillance and reconnaissance represents a monumental shift in the field of security and defense. No longer are we tethered to the limitations of human perception and interpretation. AI technology serves as a force multiplier, adding layers of analytical depth and breadth that would be impractical, if not impossible, for human agents to achieve. This technology offers the capability to sift through enormous amounts of data, distilling complex patterns and anomalies that might otherwise go unnoticed.

One of the most game-changing applications of AI lies in the deployment of unmanned aerial systems, popularly known as drones. These drones can traverse areas that are traditionally challenging for human-led operations—rugged terrains, conflict zones, or remote geographical locations. They can conduct these operations while equipped with advanced sensors and imaging devices, feeding near-real-time data back to a centralized hub. The information is then analyzed by machine learning algorithms, capable of detecting subtle movements, heat signatures, and even specific objects, providing actionable intelligence that can be crucial in time-sensitive operations.

However, the reach of AI does not stop at aerial surveillance. Ground-based systems and even underwater reconnaissance drones are adopting AI functionalities. Facial recognition technology, motion detection, and automated risk assessment are becoming standard tools in modern arsenals. The implications are especially powerful for border control and critical infrastructure protection, where the ability to rapidly identify threats can be vital.

Moreover, AI's prowess in data analytics and predictive modeling offers unprecedented advantages. For instance, machine learning can forecast potential hotspots for illegal activity based on historical and real-time data, thereby optimizing the allocation of resources. This is not just an incremental improvement but a revolutionary advance that has the potential to drastically reduce the reaction time of security forces.

However, it is crucial to navigate the ethical dimensions of AI in surveillance and reconnaissance carefully. Issues surrounding data privacy, the potential for misuse, and the need for human oversight are all valid concerns that require stringent regulations and transparent governance.

Crisis Response and Coordination

The infusion of AI into crisis response and coordination is nothing short of transformative, heralding a new era in how we manage emergencies and disasters. Traditionally, crisis management has been labor-intensive and slow, hindered by bureaucratic red tape and human error. AI's computational prowess streamlines this process, transforming disparate data into actionable insights with speed and accuracy that human operators simply cannot match.

One notable advancement is in the realm of automated communication systems. AI can efficiently synchronize efforts across multiple agencies, providing real-time updates and critical data to all stakeholders. This could be as complex as coordinating military, medical, and humanitarian efforts during a natural disaster, or as targeted as synchronizing police and emergency medical services during an act of terror. In each scenario, the end result is a unified response that maximizes the efficient use of resources and minimizes the margin of error and delay.

AI's capabilities extend even further with its ability to perform real-time analytics during a crisis situation. By assimilating data from various sources such as social media feeds, news reports, and internal agency briefings, AI algorithms can provide an ongoing situational assessment. These evaluations can then inform strategic decisions, guiding responders on everything from resource allocation to evacuation routes, often in real-time. An AI system can possibly predict the likely targets during an active terror scenario, and then automatically suggest optimal evacuation or countermeasures.

However, the rise of AI in crisis management is not without its challenges and ethical considerations. Questions surrounding data privacy, accountability, and the 'human element' in decision-making are increasingly prevalent. Just as we leverage technology to enhance our crisis response capabilities, we must also evolve our ethical frameworks and governance protocols to ensure that AI is deployed responsibly and evenly.

Ethical and Practical Considerations

While AI is unquestionably a formidable asset in counter-terrorism measures, its application is fraught with ethical ambiguities and practical complications. Consider the sensitive matter of data privacy. AI's voracious appetite for data—essential for flagging potential threats—simultaneously broaches ethical considerations when it comes to personal privacy. This forces us to reckon with a difficult question: at what point does the quest for collective security begin to erode the bedrock of individual privacy? And who gets the authority to delineate that boundary?

Accuracy is another contentious point. Despite advanced capabilities, AI systems are not immune to errors, and the specter of false positives remains a persistent concern. The stakes are not just high, they are existential. A false identification by a hyper-vigilant algorithm could have repercussions that span from simple inconvenience to grave, life-altering consequences. Further compounding the issue is the potential for AI to perpetuate existing societal biases, thereby systemically targeting specific ethnic or social groups under the banner of 'security.'

Then there is the dark scenario of these powerful technologies falling into the hands of the very entities they are designed to thwart. It is a paradoxical quandary: the tools that are key for security forces to preempt and counter terrorist actions could, in turn, be co-opted or reverse-engineered by terrorist groups. Such an eventuality would not just be ironic; it would be a catastrophic inversion, transforming a mechanism of public safety into an instrument of large-scale chaos.

Yet, despite these complexities, AI's role in counter-terrorism and public safety is undeniably transformative. It is not just a tool but a complex, multi-dimensional ally. The technology offers an array of capabilities from parsing enormous volumes of data for intelligence to powering sophisticated NLP algorithms for online monitoring. Its utility spans a spectrum that includes predictive analytics, facial recognition technologies, and cybersecurity measures. It also proves invaluable in crisis scenarios, facilitating real-time, coordinated responses to emergencies. As we traverse these complex landscapes, AI emerges as both a promising asset and a subject of ethical scrutiny. The technology not only equips us with both proactive and reactive strategies, it also challenges us to confront intricate ethical and practical issues.

Chapter 17:
Media's Double-edged Sword: Amplifying and Countering Terrorism

In today's digital age, media plays a universal role, informing, shaping, and reflecting societal values and events. But when it comes to the complex landscape of terrorism, media outlets find themselves navigating a tightrope. On one side lies the ethical and professional obligation to report events accurately and comprehensively. On the other, there is a critical responsibility to avoid becoming an unwitting conduit for extremist propaganda or exacerbating fear and panic. The very essence of terrorism is to create terror – a heightened sense of fear and vulnerability. In this context, the media's portrayal can either amplify this objective or mitigate it.

The inherent drama of terrorist acts often guarantees them a prime spot in news cycles. Bold headlines, graphic imagery, and incessant coverage can inadvertently grant terrorists the notoriety they crave, magnifying their message and influence. This overexposure can sometimes play into the hands of extremist groups, offering them a platform far larger than they might achieve on their own.

However, the media can also serve as a powerful counter-terrorism tool. By shedding light on the socio-political factors underlying terrorism, media can foster a nuanced understanding and promote dialogue over divisive rhetoric. It can debunk extremist narratives, highlight the stories of victims, and showcase the resilience and unity of communities in the face of adversity.

Striking the right balance is no small feat. Responsible reporting requires an acute awareness of the potential ramifications of every article, broadcast, or social media post. In the ever-evolving dance between media and terrorism, the challenge is to ensure that the pen (or camera) remains mightier than the sword, directing narratives towards understanding and unity, rather than division and fear.

The Oxygen of Publicity

Terrorism and the media, in the modern age, often find themselves locked in an uneasy partnership. For extremist groups, creating a spectacle is not just an incidental byproduct of their acts; it is often the very heart of their strategy. They meticulously craft high-profile attacks, leveraging the shock value of their violent acts to guarantee widespread media attention. By choosing iconic landmarks, densely populated urban hubs, or events with significant public attendance, they are not only focusing on the potential for high casualties. The real aim is to harness the symbolic importance of these sites and events to amplify their message.

This strategic targeting is not a mere coincidence. In our era of global connectivity, a single act of terror can reverberate around the world in minutes, courtesy of 24-hour news cycles and the immediacy of social media. Every news bulletin, every shared video, and every trending hashtag related to a terror act becomes a tool in the terrorist's propaganda arsenal. Such extensive coverage, even if unintentional, magnifies the impact of the attack, sowing fear, and panic far beyond the immediate scene of the crime.

Moreover, in the race to break the news first, media outlets sometimes inadvertently broadcast speculative or unverified information, adding to the chaos and confusion. As these extremists manipulate events for maximum visibility, every news segment, every shocked reaction on social media, and every front-page headline becomes part of their grim performance. Media, in its quest to inform, can unintentionally become the amplifier that broadcasts the terrorist's message to a global audience, playing directly into the hands of those who thrive on fear and division. In this, the challenge for the media becomes how to report responsibly without becoming an unwitting pawn in the terror game.

The modern media landscape, characterized by 24/7 news channels, social media live streams, and real-time updates, has brought the world closer together, yet it has also amplified the ripple effects of any major incident, including acts of terror. Continuous media coverage of terrorist events presents a complex conundrum: while the public has a right to be informed, there is a fine line between disseminating information and intensifying the intended psychological impact of the act.

Repeatedly broadcasting harrowing visuals, providing minute-by-minute updates, and speculating on possible future threats can amplify an atmosphere of panic and uncertainty. This intense focus not only retraumatizes victims and viewers but also can exaggerate the perceived frequency and imminence of such events. As the public is bombarded with the same imagery and narratives, a heightened sense of alarm and helplessness can permeate their consciousness, leading to what some experts label "terrorism fatigue" — a state of constant anxiety and fear.

Moreover, this media saturation can inadvertently bestow upon terrorists a macabre form of celebrity, allowing their messages, ideologies, and agendas to gain widespread attention. In essence, the continuous media spotlight can serve as a force multiplier for the terrorists, amplifying their reach, impact, and ability to instill fear far beyond the immediate vicinity of their actions.

The fallout is not limited to heightened public anxiety alone. The amplification effect can foster misconceptions, lead to undue stereotyping, and exacerbate divisive sentiments, especially if specific communities or groups are consistently portrayed in a negative light. The cascading consequences include potential hate crimes, social ostracization, and increased prejudice.

For media organizations, the challenge is multifaceted: How can they ensure timely, accurate, and comprehensive coverage without becoming unwitting accomplices in the terrorists' psychological warfare? It is a balance that necessitates introspection, adherence to ethical reporting standards, and a commitment to highlighting resilience, unity, and hope as fervently as the acts of terror themselves.

The Dangers of Sensationalism

In the contemporary media landscape, competition for viewership has led to an increasing trend toward sensationalism. The axiom, "If it bleeds, it leads," underscores a rather disconcerting reality of news prioritization. This sensationalist approach, especially in the context of terrorism, has profound implications on public perception and emotional well-being. One of the most conspicuous manifestations of this is the broadcasting of graphic images and the continuous looping of disturbing footage.

While these visuals might draw viewers and capture the immediacy and intensity of an event, their repeated broadcast can have deleterious effects on the audience. Each reiteration of a violent scene deepens the trauma, embedding the horrific images in the collective memory and exacerbating feelings of vulnerability. It is akin to reliving the event over and over, leading to heightened states of anxiety, distress, and even triggering post-traumatic stress in some individuals.

Beyond individual trauma, this type of media sensationalism can distort the public's perception of the frequency and magnitude of terrorist threats. A terror act, while undeniably tragic and concerning, might be isolated in nature. However, when its imagery is broadcast incessantly, it can create a perception that such events are ever-present, thereby amplifying the very climate of fear that terrorists aim to cultivate.

Furthermore, the overemphasis on violence and chaos, often at the expense of other newsworthy stories, can skew societal priorities and values. It can lead to policy decisions driven by fear rather than rationale, and a public more willing to compromise on liberties in the name of perceived safety.

For media outlets, the ethical dilemma is evident. While there is an undeniable obligation to inform the public and portray the unvarnished truth, there is an equally compelling duty to ensure that this portrayal does not inadvertently compound the harm or play into the hands of those perpetrating acts of terror. It is a delicate tightrope walk, demanding a nuanced understanding of responsibility, impact, and the greater societal good.

As news outlets find themselves in a relentless race for viewership and ratings. This mentality forces them to strive for numbers, clicks, and eyeballs and has inadvertently set the stage for a potential conflict between commercial interests and the sacred tenets of ethical journalism. While higher ratings undoubtedly translate to increased advertisement revenues and greater influence, the pursuit of these ratings can sometimes lead to a dilution of rigorous journalistic standards.
The responsibility of the media, at its core, is to inform, educate, and shed light on the truth.

However, when the pressure to be the first to break a story or to present the most sensational angle takes precedence, there is a risk of misrepresentation, oversimplification, or even misinformation. Stories might be cherry-picked based on their shock value rather than their newsworthiness or societal relevance. The depth and nuance, which are essential to understanding complex issues, may be sacrificed for catchy headlines or sensational soundbites.

Moreover, the race for ratings can amplify the more lurid aspects of a story, thereby stoking fears, perpetuating biases, or misshaping public opinion. In the context of terrorism, for instance, continuous loops of an attack, speculative reporting, or undue focus on the perpetrators rather than the victims can inadvertently magnify the terrorists' message and impact.

For news organizations, the challenge is manifold. On the one hand, they operate in a market-driven environment where ratings are paramount to survival. On the other, they are custodians of public trust, tasked with upholding the integrity of the fourth estate. Striking a balance requires introspection, a steadfast commitment to ethical journalism, and a recognition that long-term credibility and public trust are more valuable than transient spikes in viewership. In the ongoing tussle between ratings and responsibility, the latter must always guide the way.

Media's Role in Shaping Perceptions

The media wields enormous influence and power over the public's understanding of world events and societal issues. Its narratives, either consciously or subconsciously, shape the collective psyche, molding opinions, beliefs, and perceptions. However, with this power comes an immense responsibility, one that is not always judiciously upheld. Particularly in the realm of terrorism reporting, the media's portrayal can, at times, perpetuate damaging stereotypes and breed misconceptions. When acts of terror are hastily or thoughtlessly linked to specific religious or ethnic groups without nuance or context, it may inadvertently lead to generalizing and stereotyping entire communities based on the actions of a few.

Such generalizations not only perpetrate unfair biases but also foster an environment of distrust and animosity. It reduces the rich tapestry of diverse cultures and beliefs to mere caricatures, clouded by the actions of a few. When media outlets resort to sensationalist headlines or oversimplified narratives, they inadvertently deepen societal divisions, entrenching stereotypes that can take generations to dismantle. For instance, if a terrorist's religion or ethnicity is consistently emphasized without a broader context, it can create an impression that an entire community is complicit or inherently radical. This can lead to real-world consequences, from discriminatory policies to hate crimes and social ostracization.

To counteract these harmful tendencies, it is imperative for members of the media to practice conscientious reporting. This includes providing comprehensive backgrounds, avoiding unnecessary labels, and constantly challenging their own biases. By doing so, they can ensure that their role remains one of enlightenment and education rather than perpetuating division and mistrust.

Another side of the relationship between media and terrorism is the so-called "martyrdom effect" which serves as one of the most complex and contentious aspects. As media outlets strive to give comprehensive accounts of terror incidents, there is an inherent risk of inadvertently portraying terrorists in a light that's not just sympathetic, but even heroic to certain audiences. Delving deeply into a terrorist's personal history, motivations, ideologies, grievances, and struggles can humanize them, transforming them from faceless perpetrators to relatable individuals with causes, struggles, and beliefs.

For the general audience, such detailed profiles might provide a nuanced understanding of the complex factors driving individuals to commit such acts. However, for a smaller subset of the population, particularly those already harboring extremist views or those on the cusp of radicalization, these portrayals can be dangerously validating. In their eyes, the terrorist might emerge not as an extremist, but as a brave individual who stood up against perceived injustices, even if it meant paying the ultimate price. Such narratives can provide an unintended allure to the extremist path, presenting it as a righteous journey rather than a descent into violence and criminality.

Furthermore, the repetitious media coverage, which often places terrorists at the epicenter, can amplify their messages and ideologies, allowing them to reach audiences they otherwise would not have. This kind of exposure can, in essence, provide extremist groups with free propaganda platforms, with their acts and messages disseminated globally.

The challenge for media, then, becomes two-fold: How to report comprehensively without inadvertently glamorizing terrorists, and how to ensure that the broader context of terrorism – its victims, its consequences, and the efforts to combat it – does not get overshadowed by the focus on the perpetrators. In an era of rapid information dissemination and the constant hunger for exclusive content, media outlets must decide on their role in either quelling or fueling the fires of extremism.

Responsible Journalism: Counteracting Terrorism

In this rapidly evolving landscape, where sensationalism often trumps sensitivity, a new wave of responsible journalism emerges as a potent weapon against the amplification of terror. Recognizing the potential for media to inadvertently glorify perpetrators, certain media outlets have consciously decided to abstain from naming terrorists or showcasing their images. This decision strikes at the heart of what many terrorists crave: recognition and notoriety. By denying them this platform, media can diminish the appeal of terrorist acts for those seeking infamy.

Additionally, this approach shifts the narrative's focus from the attacker to the victims, humanizing those who suffered and highlighting their stories over the perpetrators'. It is a strategic recentering, spotlighting the resilience of communities and the unity that often follows these tragic events. Beyond this, such restraint by the media can prevent the spread of extremist ideologies and curb the potential for copycat acts inspired by a terrorist's newfound fame. This conscious editorial choice underscores the broader responsibility the press holds — to inform without causing harm, and to ensure that the pursuit of truth does not inadvertently further the objectives of those who seek to spread fear and division. Responsible journalism, thus, becomes not just an ethical imperative but a societal duty, vital in the collective effort to counteract the menace of terrorism.

In the aftermath of a terrorist act, while the instinctual focuses often home in on the devastation and the perpetrators, a more transformative narrative awaits — one of resilience, unity, and human spirit. Media, in its influential capacity, holds the potential to shift the spotlight to the inspiring tales of survivors, the bonds forged in adversity, and the selfless acts of heroes who emerge in the face of danger. By prioritizing these stories, the media not only honors the indomitable spirit of those affected but also presents a counter-narrative to the intended disruption and fear sought by terrorists.

This perspective does more than just inform; it inspires. It serves as a testament to human tenacity, demonstrating that even in the darkest moments, there is an inherent human drive to support, to rebuild, and to defy odds. By amplifying these stories, the media can play an instrumental role in galvanizing communities, fostering unity, and promoting a collective response that emphasizes strength over surrender, unity over division, and hope over despair. In doing so, media can effectively turn the tables, using its vast reach to undermine the very objectives of terrorism and showcase the enduring spirit of humanity.

In an era saturated with instantaneous information, the role of the media in providing accurate, verified details is more crucial than ever, especially in the context of terrorism. Recognizing this, responsible media outlets can prioritize rigorous fact-checking and refrain from speculative reporting. By ensuring that only confirmed information reaches the public, they can play a pivotal role in maintaining calm, ensuring public trust, and safeguarding against the potential manipulation of events by those with malicious intent. The commitment to truth and accuracy, in this context, becomes more than just a journalistic ethic; it emerges as a potent tool in the broader strategy to counteract the destabilizing objectives of terrorism.

Case Studies

2008 Mumbai Attacks: The 2008 Mumbai attacks, often referred to as India's 9/11, was a devastating multi-pronged assault that unfolded over three days in the heart of India's financial capital. As terrorists wreaked havoc across iconic locations in Mumbai, global and local media outlets provided near-continuous coverage, capturing every dramatic twist and turn. While this real-time reporting kept the world and the nation informed, it also sparked intense debates in the aftermath. Critics argued that the uninterrupted live broadcasts, which sometimes relayed sensitive operational details, may have inadvertently aided the terrorists and jeopardized security forces' strategic elements.

The attackers, holed up in various locations with hostages, could have potentially used the live coverage to anticipate security forces' moves.

This incident underscored the complex challenges media faces in balancing the public's right to know with the imperatives of national security. The Mumbai attacks provided a stark illustration of the unintended consequences of live media coverage during terror incidents. While the media's role is crucial in informing the public, this case highlighted the need for restraint and responsibility, ensuring that the quest for real-time information does not jeopardize security operations or amplify the terrorists' objectives.

Beslan School Hostage Crisis: In September 2004, the town of Beslan in North Ossetia, Russia, witnessed a harrowing hostage situation when armed Chechen separatists seized School Number One, taking over 1,200 hostages, predominantly children. The standoff lasted for three harrowing days, concluding in a botched rescue attempt that resulted in the tragic deaths of over 330 individuals, 186 of whom were children. The crisis was heavily covered by media outlets, with continuous live broadcasts capturing every unfolding detail. This live coverage, while informing the public, simultaneously provided tactical information about the movements and decisions of Russian security forces. Moreover, the terrorists utilized the media presence as a platform to convey their demands, ensuring a global audience for their agenda. As the crisis wore on, the struggle to present verified facts meant that misinformation and rumors riddled the broadcasts, exacerbating public anxiety and confusion.

In the aftermath, widespread criticism was aimed at the Russian media's handling of the Beslan situation. Many contended that the extensive real-time coverage might have endangered hostages further and added layers of complexity to the negotiation processes. This media scrutiny and its perceived failings prompted the Russian government to tighten its grip on national media, especially during similar security situations, a move seen by many as a method to suppress press freedom. Consequently, public trust in the media witnessed a significant decline, with the general sentiment being that accurate and responsible reporting was absent during these critical moments. The Beslan school crisis highlighted the intricate and sometimes contentious relationship between real-time media reporting and its implications during terror events, leading to a broader global conversation about the ethics of crisis journalism.

Christchurch Mosque Shootings: In March 2019, the world witnessed a harrowing act of terror in Christchurch, New Zealand, when a lone gunman targeted two mosques, leading to significant casualties. What set this attack apart was its malevolent embrace of modern technology: the attacker live-streamed his heinous act on Facebook, turning social media platforms into unwilling conduits for his extremist propaganda. The footage rapidly spread across various platforms like YouTube, Twitter, and Reddit, despite frantic efforts to remove it.

This incident not only highlighted the chilling use of technology by extremists but also brought tech giants under intense scrutiny. Questions arose about the adequacy of their content moderation policies, their ability to quickly identify and remove extremist content, and their responsibility in preventing their platforms from being weaponized by terrorists. The Christchurch attack became a grim reminder of the double-edged nature of technology. While social media can be a tool for connectivity and positivity, it can also be exploited to spread hate and terror, necessitating a renewed focus on digital vigilance and responsibility.

The incidents in Mumbai, Beslan, and Christchurch serve as stark reminders of the multifaceted challenges posed by terrorism in the digital age. These case studies highlight the unintended consequences and ethical dilemmas faced by media outlets and social media platforms when confronted with acts of terror.

In Mumbai, the media's real-time coverage unintentionally offered tactical insights to terrorists, emphasizing the need for responsible journalism that balances public awareness with operational security. Beslan's tragedy showcased the dangers of real-time reporting in volatile situations, spotlighting the media's role in potentially endangering lives while attempting to keep the public informed. The incident prompted critical discussions on media ethics and the responsibility of journalists during such crises. Meanwhile, the Christchurch mosque shooting exposed the darker side of our interconnected world, illustrating how terrorists could weaponize technology and social media platforms to amplify their heinous acts and ideologies. The rapid dissemination of the attacker's live-streamed footage highlighted the challenges tech giants face in content moderation and their broader role in preventing the spread of extremist content.

Collectively, these case studies stress the importance of reflection, responsibility, and action across media and tech sectors. In an era where information dissemination is instant, these events underscore the pressing need to strike a balance between informing the public and ensuring safety, all while maintaining the sanctity and integrity of the platforms themselves.

Chapter 18:
Counter-terrorism - Strategies and Implications

Counter-terrorism, a term both brooding and charged, has permeated global consciousness for decades now. It stands as a complex construct, touching the nerves of unease, sparking impassioned debates, and all too often, sowing the seeds of division among policymakers, security agencies, and the citizenry. If defining terrorism—a term ostensibly straightforward, yet ensnared in a thicket of ethical uncertainties and political agendas—is like navigating a minefield, then outlining the strategies for its counteraction is akin to deciphering a labyrinth inscribed with multidimensional equations.

It is not merely about identifying what terrorism is; it is about confronting an ever-shifting assemble of motivations, strategies, and tactics deployed to oppose it. This constantly evolving theater of operations compels a multi-pronged analysis. We are compelled to ask: what are the tangible mechanisms that can effectively dismantle the machinery of terror? Beyond that, what are the sociopolitical, psychological, and global repercussions of these mechanisms?

Indeed, a nuanced understanding of counter-terrorism requires delving into its various stratagems, from military interventions to intelligence operations, from psychological warfare to community outreach programs. And as we dissect these strategies, we must be fully aware of the manifest and latent implications. The former concerns the immediate and visible outcomes—lives saved, plots thwarted, terrorists apprehended. However, the latter—the indirect, long-term consequences—are often obscured by the fog of the 'here and now,' yet are just as vital to our understanding of the issue.

By drawing upon historical precedents, contemporary case studies, and future prognostications, this expanded introduction sets the stage for a multi-faceted exploration. Whether it is the fluctuating ethics of drone warfare or the efficacy of deradicalization programs; whether it is the infringement on civil liberties or the concept of 'success' in counter-terrorism efforts, our aim is to scrutinize these complex issues with the rigor and distinction they so urgently demand.

The Evolution of Counter-terrorism

The landscape of counter-terrorism has undergone seismic shifts, morphing from an era heavily reliant on intelligence-gathering and covert operations aimed at dismantling terrorist networks, to a modern theater punctuated by drone strikes, and further defined by the gentle, almost academic exercise of deradicalization programs. The progression is not merely a timeline of technological advances or a catalog of increasing options for governments to choose from. It is a paradigmatic shift in the very fabric of how societies and states conceptualize the struggle against terror.

Historically, the focus was almost exclusively on military might, intelligence operations, and law enforcement as the pillars supporting counter-terrorism efforts. Governments coordinated cloak-and-dagger operations to infiltrate terrorist groups, disrupt their activities, and apprehend or eliminate key figures. These covert initiatives were the prized horses in the race against terror, so to speak. The thinking was logical—if you could disassemble the existing terrorist networks, you could prevent their ability to wreak havoc.

In modern times, though, the set menu of strategies has expanded in remarkable ways. Authorities are now utilizing softer, more pointed methods like psychological profiling, online surveillance, and even community outreach programs aimed at integrating marginalized groups to mitigate the appeal of extremist ideologies. The fight is no longer against just the act of terror, but against the ideological and psychological seeds that, when planted in fertile ground, sprout into full-blown extremism. It is a recognition of the complex ecosystem in which terrorism takes root, acknowledging that military strikes and spy games might prune the branches but will not uproot the tree.

However, let us not idealize upon a set strategy, no matter how precise military interventions can and do result in civilian casualties. These are not mere statistics. Each number is a life lost, a family shattered, a community traumatized. And this human toll can galvanize further animosity, driving new recruits into the open arms of extremist groups. It is the classical Hydra dilemma—decapitate one head, and two more spring up in its place. The communities affected by collateral damage do not necessarily see a liberating force; they often see an invader. The cycle is self-perpetuating, a grim dance between action and reaction.

Similarly, softer approaches have their pitfalls. Deradicalization programs, though promising, are still in their infancy. Their long-term effectiveness remains a subject of ongoing research and debate. Moreover, these programs often raise ethical questions about agency, consent, and the very nature of belief. Can one truly change another's deep-seated convictions? And even if that is possible, should it be done?

The evolution of counter-terrorism is a fascinating journey through a landscape scarred by moral ambiguity, unintended consequences, and the eternal conflict between ends and means. It is a discipline forever in flux, with ever-changing rules, counter-terrorism requires a nimble mind, a robust toolkit, and a willingness to adapt and evolve. But as we forge ahead, wielding both the sword and the pen in this ceaseless struggle, we must remain ever vigilant, not just of the enemies without but also of the pitfalls and paradoxes that lie within our strategies.

The Hard vs Soft Approach

When discussing the varied approaches to counter-terrorism, one finds a distinct demarcation between "hard" and "soft" methodologies. Each approach carries its own arsenal of tools, aims, and drawbacks. Hard approaches, also known as kinetic operations, are typified by an emphasis on force and law. Here, military might, covert operations, and legislative crackdowns converge to construct an edifice of deterrence and direct action against terrorist activities. High-profile examples of such endeavors include the USA's War on Terror, which saw armed interventions within places like the Middle East and Southwest Asia, and Israel's targeted assassination campaigns aimed at neutralizing specific terrorist leaders throughout the Eastern Mediterranean area.

The immediate appeal of the hard approach is its promise of quick, decisive action. When a terrorist cell is dismantled, a leader killed, or funds frozen due to newly implemented laws, there is a palpable sense of victory, a feeling that a blow has been struck against the shadowy enemies of peace and stability. Yet, this forward-momentum often masks a vortex of ethical and practical complications that lurk behind the smokescreen of tactical gains. Civilian casualties, for example, not only pose moral quandaries but can act as catalysts for further extremism. And herein lies the ultimate question: can the hard approach ever suffice when the enemy is as much an ideology as it is a group of individuals?

Then comes the 'soft' approach, which pivots from bullets and legislations to hearts and minds. Instead of employing drones and spies, this methodology employs social workers, psychologists, and educators. Programs focusing on deradicalization, community outreach, and educational reforms are considered its crown jewels. The aim here is to drain the swamp, to confront and neutralize the ideological and emotional precursors that give rise to extremist mindsets in the first place. It seeks to build bridges where walls once stood, fostering environments that are inhospitable to extremist ideologies.

In theory, the soft approach has an elegant allure. It operates on the premise that terrorism can be eradicated not just by eliminating terrorists, but by preventing the birth of new ones. However, its effectiveness is a matter of intense debate. Critics argue that these approaches often yield slow results that are difficult to quantify. There is no ticker tape parade for the gradual process of turning potential extremists into community leaders, no dramatic footage of a drone strike taking out a terrorist training camp. But when deradicalization succeeds, when an individual transforms from a potential threat to a force for good, the soft approach proves its worth not just in gold but in lives saved, families kept whole, and communities made stronger.

It is tempting to view hard and soft approaches as mutually exclusive, but perhaps the future of effective counter-terrorism lies in a thorough integration of both. After all, while the hard approach may quash immediate threats, it is the soft approach that digs down to the root causes, offering a possibility—however tenuous—of a more enduring peace. Thus, as we continue to grapple with the challenges posed by terrorism, it behooves us to remain not only tactical but reflective, questioning not just the efficacy but the ethical dimensions of our chosen strategies. For the struggle is not just against acts of violence, but against the perpetuation of a cycle that could turn today's victories into the seeds of tomorrow's conflicts.

The Butterfly Effect: Unintended Consequences

The notion that counter-terrorism is a straightforward, linear progression of cause and effect is a tempting but perilous illusion. In reality, each move on this complex chessboard reverberates through a tangled web of consequences, often in ways that are entirely unforeseen. This intricate interplay, akin to the Butterfly Effect—a term borrowed from chaos theory—captures the essence of how a seemingly isolated action can produce ripples that eventually turn into waves, sometimes crashing disastrously on distant shores. In other words, counter-terrorism is far from a game of dominoes neatly arranged to fall just so; it is more like a cobweb where tugging on one thread of web can lead to the entire structure vibrating in unexpected ways.

Take, for example, the phenomenon of power vacuums that often emerge in the wake of military interventions. When a terrorist organization or an authoritarian regime is toppled, the immediate effect might appear to be positive. But what fills the void left behind? All too often, the collapse of a controlling power leads to a splintering of factions, each vying for control, sometimes in ways that are even more detrimental to long-term stability. The ousting of Saddam Hussein in Iraq not only destabilized the country but also contributed to the rise of new extremist entities, including ISIS. It is a scenario where the cure can be as bad, if not worse, than the disease.

Equally concerning is the stigmatization of specific communities or groups, often as a side effect of hardline policies and public discourse. Legislation that targets particular religious or ethnic communities, even under the guise of national security, can lead to widespread discrimination and marginalization. This, in turn, fuels the very extremist ideologies that such measures aim to quash. The community under scrutiny finds itself caught in a destructive cycle—marginalized by mainstream society and simultaneously more vulnerable to extremist recruitment, a double hex that compounds the original problem.

Then there are the economic ramifications, often overlooked but no less significant. The cost of maintaining a militarized approach to counter-terrorism is exorbitant, and the burden frequently falls on the ordinary taxpayer. These financial resources might be better spent addressing the root causes of extremism—be it poverty, lack of education, or social inequality. When funds are diverted from social programs to fuel military endeavors, society pays the price in more ways than one.

Moreover, the global interconnectedness in today's world further complicates the equation. Actions taken by one nation can have repercussions on international relationships, trade, and global stability. Military interventions can disrupt regional balances, leading to tensions that extend far beyond the country in question. Soft approaches, too, if mismanaged, can be weaponized by extremist propaganda to further their narrative, ironically giving them a wider platform for recruitment.

The Butterfly Effect in counter-terrorism serves as a humbling reminder that in a world of complexities and interdependencies, even the most well-intentioned strategies can produce a cascade of unintended consequences. We must remain perpetually vigilant and introspective, constantly scrutinizing not just the immediate impact of our actions, but the long-lasting ripples they send into the world.

The Ethical Morass

As the struggle against terrorism marches on, the ethical quagmire thickens. The murky intersection where civil liberties and national security meet is fraught with dilemmas that perplex even the most astute thinkers. It is as though we are navigating through a fog, where the line between protecting lives and violating rights becomes increasingly blurred. The tension between these two imperatives—security and liberty—is like an intricate dance, one wrong step, and the entire performance can come crumbling down.

Take, for instance, the pervasive surveillance programs enacted in the name of counter-terrorism. The allure is obvious: if you can monitor communications and online activities effectively, you might intercept plans for an impending attack or identify individuals at risk of radicalization. Yet, the wide net cast by these programs often ensnares innocent civilians, subjecting them to invasive scrutiny. The collective eye of state-sponsored surveillance hardly blinks, keeping tabs on phone calls, emails, and social media activity in an Orwellian panorama of watchfulness. The question then arises: what cost are we willing to pay for an illusion of complete safety?

Then there is the contentious issue of racial profiling. In airports, train stations, and even on the streets, individuals from certain ethnic or religious backgrounds find themselves excessively targeted for checks and interrogations. The rationale may seem straightforward—focus on the groups from which terrorists are most likely to emerge. But the ethical quicksand here is perilous. Profiling not only fosters resentment and alienation among innocent members of these groups but also risks overlooking threats that emanate from unexpected sectors. It is a paradox; by stigmatizing a whole community, we may create the very conditions for extremism to fester while simultaneously diverting our attention from other potential risks.

The use of torture as an interrogation technique presents yet another ethical abyss. While movies and TV shows might portray torture as a necessary evil, a means to extract life-saving information, the real-world implications are far more complex and troubling. Studies suggest that the reliability of information gained through torture is dubious at best, and the long-term damage it does to the individual and the moral standing of the perpetrating nation can be incalculable. Here again, the ethical stakes are sky-high, requiring us to grapple with questions that do not lend themselves to easy answers.

Furthermore, the ethical maze extends even into legislative chambers. Laws aimed at combating terrorism can sometimes be so sweeping that they ensnare those who are merely exercising their right to protest or voice dissent. Suddenly, an environmental activist or a vocal critic of government policy may find themselves under the lens of counter-terrorism legislation, facing penalties that are entirely out of proportion to their actions. It is as if the legislative pen, once unsheathed to combat terrorism, becomes a sword indiscriminately swung, hacking away at civil liberties.

In conclusion, the ethical landscape of counter-terrorism is far from a black-and-white tableau. It is a canvas splattered with shades of gray, each hue representing a dilemma, a compromise, or a sacrifice. As we stride forth in our battle against terrorism, it is incumbent upon us to tread carefully, ever mindful of the ethical landmines that litter our path. For in our pursuit of security, we must take care not to trample on the very ideals that form the bedrock of our society, lest we become unwitting architects of our own moral decay.

In the realm of counter-terrorism, victories are often brief, and setbacks are inescapable. The strategies employed offer a medley of benefits and detriments, with ethical, social, and political implications reverberating across dimensions we can and cannot foresee. Yet, to ignore the menace of terrorism is not an option. Perhaps the aim is not to find the ultimate solution but to engage continually in the arduous but necessary endeavor of countering terrorism. Thus, as we stand on the precipice of technological and ideological advancements, the strategies for counter-terrorism continue to be an ever-evolving tapestry, complex and intricate, forever teetering on the edge of moral and practical imperatives.

Chapter 19:
Ethical Dilemmas in Counter-terrorism - Balancing Security and Rights

As nations strive to counteract the threats of terrorism, they invariably enter a domain with profound ethical dilemmas. The central problem revolves around striking the right equilibrium between national security imperatives and the preservation of individual rights and freedoms. In a climate of heightened fear and vigilance, there is a palpable urgency to adopt robust measures, which sometimes entail increased surveillance, detentions without trial, and stringent border controls. However, these methods, while potentially effective in thwarting immediate threats, risk undermining the foundational values of democratic societies — personal liberty, privacy, and due process.

Further complicating the picture is the potential for these policies to disproportionately target specific racial, ethnic, or religious groups, leading to issues of profiling and discrimination. Such measures, if unchecked, not only erode public trust in governmental institutions but can inadvertently serve as propaganda tools for extremist groups, asserting that the 'free world' is not truly free. Thus, as nations navigate this precarious landscape, they must constantly re-evaluate their strategies, ensuring that in their pursuit of security, they do not sacrifice the very principles that define their identity and values.

Surveillance and Privacy

As the digital revolution accelerates, creating a world where communication, commerce, and even personal diaries exist in an electronic realm, nations are presented with both an opportunity and a challenge. To safeguard their populace, many governments have adopted comprehensive surveillance programs, typified by the likes of the USA's PRISM or the UK's Tempora programs. These programs are heralded by their proponents as cutting-edge mechanisms, capable of intercepting potential threats by absorbing vast swaths of internet and phone data. By being privy to a wider range of communication, intelligence agencies believe they stand a better chance at connecting the dots and preventing catastrophic events.

Yet, this coin has a flip side. The very essence of democracy is rooted in the idea of personal freedom, a space unviolated by undue governmental intervention. Critics of mass surveillance draw attention to this very principle, pointing out the inherent risks of such unchecked power. They argue that bulk data collection is not merely an inconvenience or a minor infringement, but a seismic shift in the relationship between the state and its citizens. Under the constant watchful eye of surveillance, individuals might become more hesitant to express dissenting opinions, explore alternative ideologies, or even engage in personal, confidential conversations. The 'chilling effect' of surveillance could, in essence, stifle the free discourse that is foundational to democratic societies.

Furthermore, the practical efficacy of such wide-net surveillance has also come under scrutiny. Does having more data necessarily translate to better insights, or does it merely clutter the intelligence landscape with an overwhelming volume of irrelevant information? Critics suggest that intelligence agencies might fare better with targeted surveillance, based on credible leads, rather than attempting to sieve through the daily communications of millions.

As the boundaries of what is technically possible continue to expand, democracies are faced with an existential question: How can they ensure the safety of their citizens without compromising the very liberties that define their identity? This challenge is not fleeting; it is an ongoing dialogue, requiring constant calibration and negotiation as technology and societal values evolve.

Furthermore, in today's era where data serves as both an asset and a tool of power, encryption stands as a stronghold for both privacy and protection. By converting information into coded language to ward off unauthorized scrutiny, encrypted communication has gained prominence as an essential mechanism for protecting various types of sensitive information—ranging from private dialogues and financial exchanges to secret corporate transactions. For a large number of people, encryption is considered a fundamental entitlement in our rapidly digitizing world, serving as a shield against hackers, invasive advertisers, and overreaching authorities. However, it is crucial to understand that the merits of encryption are intricately linked to the circumstances under which it is employed.

Security agencies argue that while encryption protects innocent individuals, it also offers a cloak of invisibility to malevolent actors. Terrorists, criminals, and hostile states can, and do, leverage encrypted channels to plan, communicate, and execute operations that jeopardize national security. For intelligence and law enforcement agencies, the ability to intercept and decipher such communications can be the difference between preventing a catastrophic event and reacting to its aftermath.

This dichotomy has birthed the encryption debates, which revolve around a central question: Should governments have 'backdoor' access to encrypted communications? Proponents argue that with appropriate oversight, such access can be both a shield and a sword, protecting citizens while warding off threats. They believe that a calibrated, judicially-sanctioned mechanism could strike a balance, ensuring that encryption does not become an impenetrable fortress for nefarious activities.

Detractors, however, sound the alarm on multiple fronts. Technically, introducing a 'backdoor' could create vulnerabilities, exploitable not just by governments but by hackers and adversaries. Philosophically, it raises concerns about trust: Can governments be relied upon to use such powers judiciously and not drift towards an Orwellian surveillance state? Furthermore, there is a global dimension — if one nation mandates a backdoor, others might follow suit, leading to a fragmented, insecure global communication landscape.

The encryption debate is emblematic of the broader tensions of the 21st century, where ideals of privacy, security, and technological freedom constantly intersect, challenging societies to redefine their boundaries in a mutable digital landscape.

Detention and Treatment of Suspects

Guantánamo Bay, located on the southeastern tip of Cuba, stands as a poignant testament to the complexities and moral quandaries that arose in the post-9/11 world. Originally established as a facility to house suspects believed to be associated with terrorist activities, its very existence has since spurred intense debate about the boundaries of human rights, justice, and security. For many, the name "Guantánamo" has become synonymous with indefinite detention, where individuals — some of whom were later found to have tenuous or no links to terrorism — were held without formal charges, legal representation, or the prospect of a fair trial.

The ethical concerns around Guantánamo are diverse. Foremost is the principle of habeas corpus, a cornerstone of democratic legal systems that protects against arbitrary detention. This right was effectively suspended for many detainees, raising questions about the erosion of foundational legal norms in the face of security threats. Additionally, harrowing accounts of enhanced interrogation techniques — labeled by many as torture — further muddied the waters. Such practices, critics argue, not only violate international human rights standards but also diminish the moral standing of nations that uphold themselves as beacons of justice and liberty.

Additionally, the mere existence of Guantánamo, situated outside the mainland U.S., appeared to some as a deliberate attempt to circumvent legal jurisdictions and norms. For many observers, this off-shore detention strategy exemplified a "grey zone" approach to justice, where the traditional rules did not apply, and the lines between right and wrong became blurred.

In grappling with the legacy of Guantánamo Bay, societies are forced to confront challenging questions: Can the imperatives of national security ever justify the suspension of fundamental rights? And if so, at what cost? These inquiries underscore the perpetual tension between safeguarding citizens and preserving the moral and ethical values that form the bedrock of democratic societies.

In the aftermath of grave terror attacks, nations grapple with the pressing demand to extract information that could preempt future threats. This urgency led to the adoption of what were termed "enhanced interrogation techniques" by some security agencies. Among these, 'waterboarding' stands out as one of the most controversial methods. Proponents argue that such techniques are indispensable tools in the arsenal of counter-terrorism, claiming their use has sometimes yielded valuable intelligence. Critics, however, vehemently decry these methods as torture, both ethically indefensible and legally proscribed under international law.

The very terminology, "enhanced interrogation," is seen by many as an Orwellian euphemism, a calculated attempt to sanitize practices that, in any other context, would be labeled as torture. Beyond the moral questions, many experts challenge the efficacy of these techniques. They contend that information elicited under extreme duress is often unreliable, as detainees might say anything to end their suffering, leading to potential misinformation. Moreover, the use of torture carries profound implications for a nation's global standing. Countries that once positioned themselves as champions of human rights find their credibility eroded when they resort to practices reminiscent of oppressive regimes.

In a broader perspective, the debate over enhanced interrogation techniques reflects deeper existential questions: In striving to protect the physical well-being of citizens, to what extent can nations compromise the very values that define their moral fabric? And does the potential gain in security justify the undeniable cost to a nation's conscience and international reputation? As societies grapple with these dilemmas, they are confronted with the challenging task of navigating the fine line between ensuring safety and upholding the sanctity of human dignity.

Targeted Killings and Drone Strikes

In the technologically advanced age of warfare, drone strikes have emerged as a preferred method for neutralizing perceived threats, especially in regions where 'boots-on-the-ground' operations are deemed too risky or politically unfeasible. These unmanned aerial vehicles, often armed with precision missiles, can target specific individuals or structures with a degree of accuracy that minimizes the risk to combatants. However, this technological marvel comes with its own set of ethical quandaries.

While drones can be surgically precise, the intelligence guiding them is only as good as its sources. Misinformation or misinterpretation can lead to tragic mistakes, resulting in the loss of innocent civilian lives, often termed as "collateral damage." Each such incident not only represents a profound human tragedy but also serves to further alienate local populations, potentially fueling anti-west sentiments and providing extremist groups with potent propaganda material.

The ethical concerns are further compounded by the nature of drone warfare. The detachment of launching strikes from thousands of miles away, often from the safety of a remote base, raises questions about the dehumanization of warfare. When the act of taking a life becomes as clinical as a video game, does it lower the threshold for lethal action?

The debate surrounding drone strikes is emblematic of the broader challenges in modern counter-terrorism. As nations strive to protect their citizens, they must continually evaluate the moral, strategic, and long-term implications of their actions. The challenge lies in harnessing the capabilities of advanced weaponry while remaining acutely conscious of the human and ethical costs inherent in their use.

In the dynamic and often murky theater of counter-terrorism, the practice of extrajudicial killings, or the deliberate targeting of individuals deemed to be threats without the due process of a trial, remains one of the most controversial strategies. While such actions might be framed as pragmatic or even necessary in the face of imminent threats, they carry with them profound implications for international law, human rights, and the foundational tenets of justice.

First and foremost, executing operations to neutralize persons within foreign lands, without the clear approval of the respective sovereign state, fundamentally contradicts the tenets of national sovereignty. These actions can put diplomatic ties at risk, possibly upsetting the equilibrium of regional power dynamics and eroding the foundations of global collaboration. Additionally, the lack of a transparent legal procedure implies that judgments are frequently grounded in intelligence data. While this information may be valid, it does not undergo the meticulous examination that would be required in a judicial setting.

Furthermore, these killings can inadvertently turn targets into martyrs, making them symbols for extremist propaganda and potentially galvanizing further radicalization. The danger here is twofold: not only does this potentially swell the ranks of extremist factions, but it also erodes the moral high ground that democracies claim in their fight against terror.

While extrajudicial killings might offer short-term tactical advantages, they pose significant long-term strategic, ethical, and legal challenges.

The debate surrounding their use underscores the intricate and often paradoxical choices nations face in their pursuit of security, especially when confronting non-traditional and asymmetric threats.

Citizenship and Exile

The concept of citizenship, intrinsically linked to identity, rights, and belonging, has found itself at the epicenter of debates concerning counter-terrorism strategies. In an effort to combat the return of individuals involved in extremist activities abroad, certain nations have begun considering or even implementing measures to revoke the citizenship of such individuals. This approach, while seemingly an effective deterrent on the surface, unravels a web of intricate legal, ethical, and human rights considerations.

Firstly, the act of stripping someone of their citizenship can inadvertently render them stateless if they do not possess dual citizenship, which directly contravenes international conventions such as the 1961 Convention on the Reduction of Statelessness. Being stateless not only deprives one of basic rights and protections but can also leave the individual in a void, often stuck between countries and in perpetual legal limbo.

Moreover, the revocation of citizenship without a transparent and robust judicial process can be perceived as a punitive measure that bypasses the principles of due process. This raises ethical concerns about whether it is just to exile individuals based on suspicion or association rather than concrete evidence. The potential for mistakes or misuse of this policy looms large, with potential ramifications for innocent individuals.

Lastly, there is a broader, societal implication to consider: when a state chooses exile over reintegration or justice within its legal framework, it may be seen as abdicating its responsibility to rehabilitate or punish its citizens. By pushing the problem elsewhere, it potentially magnifies the risk on a global scale, rather than containing and addressing it.

Even though revoking citizenship might seem like a straightforward solution to a complex problem, it is a tactic fraught with profound consequences that ripple across legal, ethical, and humanitarian dimensions. The balance between national security and fundamental human rights remains a challenging tightrope to walk, especially in the dynamic and evolving landscape of global terrorism.

Balancing Act: National Security vs. Civil Liberties

Navigating the perplexities between national security and civil liberties has always been a complex endeavor, made even more intricate in the context of a rapidly changing global threat landscape. At the heart of this balance lies the pressing need to protect a nation and its citizens from the looming specter of terrorism while ensuring that the very freedoms and principles that define democratic societies are not compromised. Enacting robust security laws can undoubtedly act as a bulwark against potential threats, providing governments with tools and powers that can preemptively thwart terror plots and bring perpetrators to justice.

However, this protective shield, when unchecked, can double as a sword. The potential for misuse is significant, especially when laws are crafted with broad strokes that grant sweeping powers. There lies the risk of these laws being weaponized to stifle legitimate dissent, silence opposition, or target specific communities under the guise of national security. History bears witness to instances where authorities, armed with such laws, have profiled, surveilled, and even unjustly detained individuals based on ethnicity, religion, or political beliefs rather than concrete evidence of malicious intent.

Additionally, the perception of these laws, especially if they are seen as disproportionately affecting certain groups, can further alienate those communities. This not only sows' seeds of distrust and fear but can inadvertently fan the flames of radicalization, leading to a counterproductive cycle. In essence, the quest for security should not be at the expense of the very liberties and principles nations seek to protect. Striking this balance demands rigorous oversight, transparent legal processes, and an unwavering commitment to upholding the rights and dignity of every individual.

In an era marked by heightened threats and recurrent terror incidents, the collective psyche of societies has been profoundly impacted. Fear, a primal and potent emotion, often becomes the lens through which citizens view national security measures. When confronted with the looming specter of a terror attack, the public's yearning for safety and security can overshadow concerns about individual freedoms and rights. This heightened state of anxiety can make societies more malleable to policies and measures that, under more tranquil circumstances, might be met with skepticism or outright opposition.

Government actions that involve increased surveillance, stringent security checks, or even curbs on certain freedoms can be perceived as necessary evils in the quest to safeguard national interests. The rationale is straightforward: if such measures can prevent even a single terror incident, then the trade-offs, however uncomfortable, are worth it. However, this perspective, driven by genuine fear, can sometimes be exploited. Governments may push forward policies that not only address immediate threats but also consolidate power or suppress dissenting voices. It is a delicate maneuver where genuine concern for citizen safety can become intertwined with more Machiavellian political strategies.

For democracies, this dynamic presents a unique challenge. They must continually ensure that the voice of the public, shaped by the realities of a post-9/11 world, is heard and respected while also upholding the foundational principles of freedom and individual rights. It underscores the importance of informed public discourse, transparent decision-making, and vigilant oversight in shaping counter-terrorism policies.

Understanding these ethical dilemmas is essential for any democratic society. It prompts introspection on the nature of freedom, the value of individual rights, and the lengths to which governments should go to protect their citizens. Conversely, an overtly laissez-faire approach, one that prioritizes absolute freedom without adequate safeguards, may leave a nation vulnerable to threats, compromising the very freedom it seeks to uphold. This paradox underscores the intricate balancing act that governments must perform.

In this endeavor, open dialogue is crucial. Engaging with citizens, understanding their fears, aspirations, and concerns, and educating them about the complexities of national security can create a more informed and understanding populace. Only through such transparent and inclusive discussions can societies chart a path that upholds and safeguards individual rights while ensuring the collective security of the nation.

Chapter 20:
International Law and Prosecution of Terrorists

The comprehensive arena of global legal action against terrorists is underpinned by a range of conventions, resolutions, and agreements that span both bilateral and multilateral partnerships. Instruments like various UN conventions and protocols address specific kinds of terrorist activities, from hijackings and hostage situations to bombings. This summary seeks to illuminate these international norms, highlighting their crucial role in establishing a consistent foundation for collective action against terrorism.

Yet, these conventions are not without their challenges, particularly when it comes to extradition. Nations often diverge in their legal systems, evidentiary rules, and even in defining what constitutes a "terrorist act." Added to this are the legal and ethical dilemmas surrounding human rights, including the right to a fair trial and the prohibition against torture. This discourse explores these complexities, from the limitations of Mutual Legal Assistance Treaties (MLATs) to the ethical considerations and notable case studies that illuminate both the achievements and shortcomings of international counter-terrorism efforts. It also delves into the ongoing dialogue about the feasibility of a dedicated international court for terrorism, evaluating its potential benefits and inherent challenges.

Challenges of Prosecuting Terrorists across International Borders

The challenges of prosecuting international terrorists are multi-faceted and complex, with jurisdictional conflicts at the forefront. Determining which country has the rightful authority to prosecute terrorists who commit crimes in multiple regions poses intricate questions. While the principle of 'territoriality' posits that states can prosecute crimes within their borders, the fluidity of terrorism often tests these delineations. Moreover, the process of extradition, where a country seeks the return of an individual to face charges, introduces its own set of dilemmas. States may be hesitant due to political affiliations with the alleged criminal's homeland, and variations in legal definitions of terrorism across countries further complicate matters. The apprehension that a suspect may endure torture or an unjust trial in the petitioning nation can also inhibit extradition.

Evidence sharing, vital for prosecuting terrorists, also bears its challenges. Countries might withhold intelligence, wary of exposing confidential sources or methods. Additionally, the diversity in legal standards across nations can lead to discrepancies, as evidence permissible in one country might be rejected in another, thereby complicating joint prosecutions. International collaboration, while pivotal, confronts obstacles too. Historic disputes or diplomatic strains can obstruct effective cooperation between countries. In addition, differences in technological expertise, training, and resources can create gaps in tracing and capturing suspects.

A notable impediment in the extradition process is the principle of dual criminality, which dictates that for a person to be extradited, their act must be deemed criminal in both involved nations. This becomes problematic when specific acts of terrorism are not universally recognized as crimes. Furthermore, terrorists frequently exploit regions with weaker governance, using them as 'safe havens'. This exploitation poses challenges for nations with stringent legal structures aiming to apprehend and prosecute these individuals. The digital age, marked by the surge of cyber-terrorism, adds layers of complexity to this already intricate landscape. Digital evidence may be stored on servers in third countries, demanding more comprehensive cooperation and legal strategies to access.

Role of International Legal Frameworks and Conventions

As global threats evolve, the necessity for a collective response becomes more pronounced. The rise of transnational terrorism exemplifies this demand, leading to the increased prominence of international legal frameworks and conventions in the fight against it. Central to their effectiveness is their ability to bridge disparities between national legislations, carving pathways for cooperation to tackle the intricacies of terrorism head-on.

Among the most influential instruments in this domain are the United Nations Security Council Resolutions (UNSCR). The UNSCRs, over the years, have crafted a comprehensive agenda against terrorism. These resolutions not only assist in formulating a universally accepted definition of terrorism, reducing ambiguity among member states but also levy sanctions on countries, organizations, and individuals entwined with terrorist activities. Such measures exert economic and political pressure, curbing their operations. Furthermore, many of these resolutions come with a binding effect, compelling member nations to act against terror financing, fortify border security, and actively partake in intelligence sharing.

Another significant convention is the International Convention for the Suppression of Acts of Nuclear Terrorism (ICSANT). Recognizing the calamitous implications of nuclear terrorism, the ICSANT was birthed to thwart potential nuclear terrorist acts and ensure that the culprits face prosecution and punishment. The convention accentuates mutual cooperation, emphasizing the criticality of sharing information and aiding each other in investigations and extradition. It also delineates specific offenses, particularly those revolving around the possession and usage of radioactive materials with malevolent intent. Furthermore, a salient feature of the ICSANT is its focus on safeguarding radioactive substances, preventing their acquisition by malicious forces.

Merging with the UNSCR and ICSANT are other conventions, nestled under the expansive umbrella of the United Nations. Conventions like the International Convention for the Suppression of the Financing of Terrorism and the International Convention against the Taking of Hostages are testament to this multi-pronged approach. These conventions have distinct but interwoven objectives: to universally criminalize particular acts thereby constricting the operational space for terrorists, to amplify judicial cooperation ensuring that terrorists find no refuge, and to bolster the counter-terrorism capacities of individual countries, promoting a harmonized global response.

The potency of these international frameworks and conventions is undeniable. Though they grapple with implementation hurdles, primarily stemming from divergent national interests and definitions, their essence lies in fostering unity. They facilitate standardization, galvanize cooperation, and apply pressure on non-compliant stakeholders, solidifying the global counter-terrorism framework. Their very existence is a testament to the international community's firm commitment to eradicating the scourge of terrorism.

Prospects and Obstacles of Establishing an International Court for Terrorism

Establishing an international court for terrorism-related crimes is an intriguing proposition that has often been the centerpiece of global legal debates. The merits of creating such a specialized tribunal are manifold. Primarily, a dedicated court would house experts with a deep understanding of the intricacies of terrorism, leading to more nuanced judgments. This expertise would translate to a consistent, standardized approach to cases, potentially reducing the discrepancies that sometimes arise from varying national interpretations of terrorism. Moreover, such a court could serve as a beacon of justice, signaling the global community's unified stance against acts of terror, and possibly deterring potential offenders with its very existence.

However, the path to actualizing this idea is riddled with challenges. Political considerations loom large. Nations, driven by their strategic interests, might perceive such a court as an impingement on their sovereignty or fear its misuse for political vendettas. Jurisdictional concerns further complicate the picture. Determining the reach and authority of this court and reconciling it with national jurisdictions would be an enormous task. Furthermore, the objective of ensuring universal support appears elusive. The disparities in how nations define, and approach terrorism means that a one-size-fits-all court could face resistance, with some countries fearing undue prosecution or influence. Lastly, logistical issues, such as funding and hosting the court, could generate further contention among nations.

While the idea of an international court dedicated to terrorism-related crimes offers a promising avenue to streamline global counter-terrorism efforts, the array of political, jurisdictional, and logistical challenges makes its establishment a complex endeavor. The realization of such a court, hinges on striking a balance between global cooperation and respecting national sensibilities, a task that demands both diplomatic finesse and unwavering commitment.

The imperative to bring terrorists to justice is undeniably robust. The global community's collective conscience demands that those who commit heinous acts face accountability. Yet, in the fervor to prosecute, there lies a parallel duty: the obligation to uphold the sacrosanct principles of justice. The intersection of these twin goals—accountability and justice—creates a complex maze through which international legal mechanisms must carefully tread.

A primary challenge is evidence gathering. Acts of terrorism often leave behind scenes of devastation, making it difficult to extract irrefutable evidence. Moreover, the evidence often spans across national borders, ensnared in webs of differing jurisdictions and legal protocols. While some nations might willingly share intelligence, others might withhold critical information, fearing diplomatic repercussions or the exposure of covert operations. How does one ensure that the evidence, once presented in court, has been obtained ethically, without resorting to torture or other illicit means?

Legal representation offers another quandary. In a world where certain individuals are quickly branded as "terrorists," can they be assured impartial legal defense? It is a fundamental tenet of justice that every accused, regardless of the severity of their purported crime, has the right to a defense. Yet, lawyers representing those accused of terrorism might face threats, stigmatization, or professional ostracization. The international community must grapple with how to protect these legal practitioners, ensuring that they can operate without fear or prejudice.

Due process, the cornerstone of any fair legal system, assumes paramount importance in cases of transnational terrorism. The accused must be given a fair chance to contest the charges, be informed of their rights, and be tried without undue delay. In the global arena, where multiple legal systems with differing definitions of due process come into play, standardizing these protections is a formidable task. Further, there is the risk of "secret trials" or "military tribunals," which might shun standard judicial procedures in the name of national security.

Additionally, respecting human rights is non-negotiable. International conventions underscore the inviolability of these rights, even for those accused of grave crimes. Yet, instances of extrajudicial killings, forced disappearances, and torture continue to surface, blurring the lines between justice and retribution.

Case Studies

The Lockerbie Bombing Trial (2000): In 1988, a tragic event occurred when Pan Am Flight 103 exploded over Lockerbie, Scotland, resulting in the deaths of all 259 people on board and an additional 11 individuals on the ground. Investigations soon revealed the involvement of two Libyan intelligence officers. Following years of intense diplomatic negotiations and the imposition of sanctions against Libya, the suspects were eventually surrendered for prosecution. Interestingly, the trial was held in the Netherlands but was conducted under Scottish law.

Ultimately, Abdelbaset al-Megrahi was convicted and sentenced to life imprisonment, while his co-accused was acquitted. This entire episode underscored the power and potential of international collaboration in combating terrorism. The unique approach of utilizing a third-country jurisdiction for the trial, combined with the overarching geopolitical challenges, provided a notable lesson on the complexities and possibilities inherent in international counter-terrorism efforts.

The Trial of Hambali (ongoing as of January 2023): Riduan Isamuddin, commonly known as Hambali, was identified as the orchestrator of the devastating 2002 Bali bombings, a tragedy that claimed the lives of 202 people. In a turn of events in 2003, he was apprehended in Thailand and has since been detained in Guantanamo Bay. Despite over 17 years of detention, military prosecutors have indicated that a comprehensive trial for Hambali and his two co-accused might only commence in March 2025. This prolonged pre-trial detention underscores the intricate challenges associated with prosecuting suspects housed in places like Guantanamo Bay. It raises pressing ethical questions surrounding the manner in which evidence is gathered and the broader implications of extended incarcerations without a formal trial.

The Trial of "Carlos the Jackal" (1990s - 2010s): During the 1970s and 1980s, Ilich Ramírez Sánchez, infamously known as "Carlos the Jackal," became one of the most sought-after terrorists globally. He orchestrated a series of bombings, assassinations, and hostage situations primarily aimed at Western entities, with his reign of terror extending across nations like France, the UK, Germany, and Israel. Yet, after years of successfully evading authorities, his run came to an end in 1994 when he was arrested in Sudan and subsequently extradited to France.

In a landmark trial in 1997, Ramírez was handed a life sentence for the murder of two French intelligence officers and an informant. This was only the beginning, as further trials in 2011 and 2017 convicted him of additional attacks in France, resulting in more life sentences. The journey to bring "Carlos the Jackal" to justice showcased the perseverance of intelligence agencies and the critical role international collaboration plays in counter-terrorism. Assembling evidence for his myriad crimes was a daunting task, given their spread over different countries and timelines. Yet, his prosecution illustrated the possibility of achieving justice for acts of terror, no matter how dated. The media's vast coverage of Carlos raised awareness about the complexities of terrorism but also prompted ethical debates on the potential glorification of such figures and the media's influence on the justice system.

The East Africa Embassy Bombings Trial (2001): In 1998, a devastating act by Al-Qaeda led to the bombing of US embassies in Kenya and Tanzania, resulting in the tragic loss of over 200 lives. Following the attacks, a swift international response saw the capture and extradition of several suspects to the United States. When put on trial in New York, four of the men were found guilty on charges of terrorism and conspiracy. This entire process underscored two pivotal insights: the integral role of international teamwork in evidence collection and the capability of civilian courts in effectively prosecuting terrorists.

These case studies, while representing just a fraction of global terrorism prosecutions, illuminate the maze of challenges and considerations in cross-border trials. They emphasize the criticality of international cooperation, the importance of adhering to human rights and legal principles, and the persistent tug-of-war between geopolitics and justice. Each trial provides valuable takeaways, forming a blueprint for future prosecutions and underscoring the importance of unity and tenacity in the face of global threats.

As the world continues to grapple with the evolving threat of terrorism, the international legal mechanisms designed to counteract these threats are similarly undergoing transformations. The future of international counter-terrorism legal mechanisms will be defined not only by the restructuring of existing frameworks but also by the development of novel strategies to tackle unprecedented challenges.

One of the primary avenues for progress lies in the possibility of enhanced international collaboration. Driven by the common goal of maintaining global stability, nations could be incentivized to adopt more harmonized strategies that seal legal loopholes and eliminate possible sanctuaries for terrorists. This could entail more efficient procedures for extradition, reciprocal legal support, and the collective use of databases that hold details on individuals suspected of terrorism.

The rise of cyberterrorism represents one of the more formidable challenges on the legal horizon. As terrorists leverage the digital realm to carry out attacks, recruit members, and disseminate propaganda, the international community must adapt its legal tools accordingly. This entails not only classifying cyber-attacks as terroristic acts but also ensuring the capacity to trace, attribute, and prosecute such acts. Cyber legal frameworks will need to account for the nebulous nature of digital space, where actors can hide behind layers of anonymity and operate across borders with ease.

Moreover, as technology continues to advance, the possibility of new forms of terroristic threats—such as those involving artificial intelligence, drones, or bio-terrorism—cannot be ruled out. Proactively, international legal mechanisms will need to anticipate these shifts, ensuring that they are equipped to deal with threats that were once the stuff of science fiction. The future of international counter-terrorism legal mechanisms lies in their ability to be both reactive and proactive. While they must continue to address and learn from past and current challenges, they also need to be forward-thinking, preparing for and mitigating threats that are yet to emerge.

Chapter 21:
The Role of Education in Countering Terrorism

Education serves as a formidable instrument for combatting terrorism by encouraging critical thinking and instilling values that oppose extremist ideologies. Beyond mere knowledge transfer, comprehensive educational programs can cultivate the principles of tolerance, diversity, and mutual respect, thereby undermining the separatist narratives that often fuel terrorist motivations. As we explore this subject, we will delve into the various ways education can both act as a preventive measure against the pull of radicalization and actively work to dismantle such narratives.

At the grassroots, schools serve as spaces where young minds are exposed to varied perspectives, encouraging them to think critically and question oversimplified or complex views. Curricula that prioritize global citizenship, inclusivity, and conflict resolution can be instrumental in immunizing the younger generation against the appeal of radical ideologies. Moreover, in regions scarred by strife and conflict, education can offer a semblance of normalcy, providing youths with opportunities and aspirations beyond the confines of their immediate circumstances.

Beyond formal education, lifelong learning and community-based educational programs can play pivotal roles in de-radicalizing individuals who may have already been exposed to extremist views. Such interventions, grounded in dialogue and understanding, can rehabilitate and reintegrate individuals, redirecting them towards constructive societal roles.

However, the transformative potential of education also comes with its challenges. Issues like ensuring universal access to quality education and averting the risk of schools becoming breeding grounds for radicalization present significant challenges. As we delve into these various dimensions, it becomes clear that in the global struggle against terrorism, a well-directed educational effort can, in fact, prove more potent than any arsenal.

The Power of Education in Preventing Radicalization

Radicalization often stems from feelings of disenfranchisement, simplistic narratives that appeal to emotions, and the human tendency to seek belonging and purpose. Against this backdrop, education emerges as a potent antidote, acting as both a preventive and rehabilitative force. Through its layered nature, education shapes not just an individual's academic prowess but their very ethos, their capacity for empathy, and their ability to critically evaluate information.

One of the primary ways educations build resilience against extremist narratives is by nurturing critical thinking skills. In an era of information overload, the ability to discern fact from fiction, to challenge prevailing narratives, and to question one's own biases becomes paramount. Schools and colleges can become sanctuaries where students are taught not what to think, but how to think. This cognitive armor acts as a bulwark against propaganda and simplistic extremist ideologies.

Furthermore, education fosters empathy and understanding. By exposing students to diverse histories, cultures, and perspectives, it challenges insular views and cultivates an appreciation for humanity's shared experiences and aspirations. When classrooms become microcosms of the broader world, students learn to recognize the shared humanity that binds them to their peers, diminishing the appeal of ideologies that thrive on divisiveness and hatred.

Promoting open dialogue is another critical facet of education's power. Spaces where students feel safe to voice their opinions, ask questions, and engage in constructive debates become incubators for tolerance and mutual respect. These dialogues serve to demystify 'the other,' breaking down barriers and challenging stereotypes.

In essence, while extremist narratives often prey on vulnerabilities, be they emotional, cognitive, or social, a robust educational foundation equips individuals and their peers with the tools to dissect, challenge, and resist these narratives. As we navigate this topic, we will unearth the various ways through which education not only imparts knowledge but serves as a beacon, illuminating a path away from the shadows of radicalization.

Integrating Counter-terrorism Education into Curricula

The classroom serves as a nexus for molding young minds, making it a critical battleground in the war against radical ideologies and extremism.

Recognizing this, the idea of embedding counter-terrorism education within the curriculum has gained traction in many educational circles. However, the integration of such content is not merely about teaching students about terrorism; it is about fostering a holistic understanding that allows them to critically evaluate extremist narratives and understand the multitude of different drivers of terrorism.

One effective approach is embedding counter-terrorism discussions within broader subjects. For instance, history lessons can trace the origins of extremist groups, dissecting their motivations, strategies, and evolutions over time. This provides context and highlights the cyclical nature of such movements. Meanwhile, social science courses can delve into the sociopolitical conditions that often serve as breeding grounds for radical ideologies, emphasizing the complex interplay of factors that might lead individuals down extremist paths.

Literature and media studies classes can be instrumental in dissecting propaganda techniques. By examining extremist literature, videos, and online posts, students can gain insights into the emotional and psychological tactics employed to recruit and radicalize individuals. They can then be taught to counteract these techniques, cultivating a level of media literacy tailored to the digital age's challenges.

However, integrating counter-terrorism into the curriculum is not without its challenges. There is the risk of inadvertently stigmatizing certain groups if not approached with sensitivity and inclusivity. Teachers need adequate training to handle discussions maturely, avoiding bias and ensure that the dialogue is constructive rather than fear-inducing. Furthermore, age-appropriateness is crucial. While older students may benefit from in-depth discussions, younger ones may require a more abstract values-based approach that emphasizes peace, unity, and understanding.

There are evident advantages to this approach, though. A well-implemented counter-terrorism curriculum can promote tolerance, dispel misconceptions, and make students more discerning consumers of information. They become less susceptible to extremist propaganda and more empowered to challenge such narratives among their peers.

While the prospect of integrating counter-terrorism into educational curricula might seem daunting, it offers an invaluable opportunity. By engaging with the topic head-on, educators can equip their students with the cognitive and emotional tools needed to navigate a world where extremist ideologies, unfortunately, persist. Through knowledge, understanding, and critical thinking, students can become the vanguards against extremism's allure.

Empowering Teachers and Parents to Recognize Signs of Radicalization

During the journey of upbringing and education, teachers and parents often serve as the primary beacons, guiding the youth away from the pitfalls of radicalization. These individuals have a unique vantage point, given their close and sustained interactions with young minds. Their potential to recognize early signs of extremist leanings can be the difference between timely intervention and missed opportunity.

Recognizing signs of radicalization is not solely about observing overt behaviors like espousing extremist views or justifying violence. Often, it is the subtler shifts that give cause for concern: sudden changes in social circles, withdrawal from family and friends, heightened secrecy about online activities, or consuming extremist content. Educators, given their daily interaction with students, might notice a pronounced shift in a student's demeanor, the choice of topics for assignments, or even the nature of doodles on a notebook.

However, this vigilance necessitates robust training. Workshops and seminars for educators that highlight the nuances of radicalization, its driving factors, and the difference between a fleeting adolescent phase and genuine concern are paramount. Such training should be culturally sensitive, ensuring that teachers do not inadvertently profile or stigmatize certain groups through biases. It should also be recurrent, adapting to the ever-evolving strategies of extremist recruiters.

Parents, on the other hand, require a different kind of guidance. Their deep emotional connection with their children can sometimes act as a hinderance: while it offers them intuitive insights into their child's state of mind, it can also lead to denial or misinterpretation of warning signs. Parental workshops can focus on open communication strategies, age-appropriate digital supervision, and fostering trust, ensuring children feel comfortable sharing their online and offline experiences.

Creating safe spaces for dialogue is equally crucial. Schools should foster an environment where controversial topics can be discussed maturely. Debating clubs, open forums, or moderated discussion groups can provide students an outlet to voice their opinions, however contrarian, under the guidance of a trained educator. Similarly, parents should be encouraged to cultivate a home environment where questions and curiosities, no matter how unsettling, can be addressed without fear of reprimand.

In essence, the fight against radicalization begins in classrooms and living rooms. By empowering educators and parents with the knowledge and tools to recognize and address early signs of extremist leanings, we bolster our first line of defense, ensuring that vulnerable individuals receive guidance and support before they tread down a perilous path.

Challenges and Controversies in Teaching Counter-terrorism

Introducing counter-terrorism into the educational sphere is a commendable endeavor, but it brings with it a myriad of challenges and contentious issues. Venturing into this domain means treading a delicate balance, one that takes into consideration the diverse perspectives and sensitivities that surround the subject.

Firstly, there is the inherent risk of bias. How can educators present a neutral stance on subjects that often have deeply rooted political, religious, and cultural implications? The materials selected for the curriculum, the manner in which topics are discussed, and even the language used can inadvertently reinforce stereotypes or offer a skewed portrayal of certain groups. This bias, if unchecked, could ironically contribute to the very radicalization this education aims to prevent.

Censorship is another area of concern. Deciding what content is deemed appropriate for students can be a slippery slope. Should graphic events be discussed? Where does one draw the line between raising awareness and exposing students to traumatic details? Furthermore, attempting to sanitize or oversimplify complex issues can lead to a superficial understanding, defeating the purpose of rounded education on the subject.

Then comes the ethical quagmire. Some argue that integrating counter-terrorism into education may infringe on the rights and privacy of students. Surveillance or monitoring of students' reactions, opinions, or behaviors, even if well-intentioned, can be perceived as invasive. Additionally, there is the danger of creating a climate of suspicion, where students feel they are constantly under scrutiny and therefore become reluctant to voice genuine questions or concerns.

Moreover, the age-appropriateness of counter-terrorism discussions is a significant debate. What might be suitable for a university seminar could be deeply disturbing for a younger audience. Ensuring that the content aligns with the emotional and cognitive maturity of the students is crucial.

Lastly, there is the international dimension to consider. Counter-terrorism narratives differ globally based on regional histories, geopolitics, and cultural contexts. What is taught in one country might be viewed as contentious or even offensive in another. Finding a universally acceptable narrative is nearly impossible, yet understanding these divergent perspectives is essential for a comprehensive grasp of the subject.

Recognizing these challenges does not mean shying away from the topic. Instead, it necessitates a thoughtful and informed approach. Engaging in continuous dialogue with educators, students, parents, and experts in the field can pave the way for a curriculum that is both sensitive and informative. Through collaborative efforts, the goal is to cultivate a generation equipped to understand, question, and ultimately counteract the forces of radicalization and extremism.

Case Studies of Educational Initiatives Against Terrorism

Educational programs geared toward countering terrorism have been launched worldwide, demonstrating the versatility and impact of scholastic tools. These initiatives, ranging from grassroots efforts to nationwide campaigns, provide illuminating examples of education's potential as a counter-radicalization tool.

Pakistan - Sabaoon Rehabilitation Center: Located in the Swat Valley, Sabaoon is a school and rehabilitation center for boys formerly involved with extremist groups. The center combines formal education with psychosocial counseling, sports, and arts. Through a personalized approach, the facility helps reintegrate these children back into society. The Sabaoon model underlines the power of complete interventions in addressing root causes of radicalization.

Denmark - Aarhus Model: The city of Aarhus pioneered a de-radicalization program that hinges on cooperation between the police, social services, and schools. Teachers are trained to recognize signs of radicalization, and instead of criminalizing the youth, they are provided with mentorship opportunities, counseling, and educational support. The program's success has been attributed to its emphasis on reintegration over punishment.

United Kingdom - Prevent Strategy: A more controversial example is the UK's Prevent strategy, which aims to prevent people from becoming terrorists or supporting terrorism. Central to this is the 'Channel' program, where educators, along with health and social care professionals, refer individuals showing signs of radicalization for intervention support. While it has seen successes, it also faced criticisms for potentially stigmatizing Muslim communities.

Nigeria - Safe Schools Initiative: Launched in response to attacks on schools by extremist groups, this initiative aims to make schools safer and integrate peace education into the curriculum. Students are taught conflict resolution, critical thinking, and the importance of tolerance and coexistence. By fostering these values early on, the program hopes to deter youth from joining extremist factions.

Indonesia - Pesantren Against Radicalism: Indonesia has harnessed the influence of its traditional Islamic boarding schools, or pesantren, to combat extremist ideologies. Several pesantrens have revamped their curricula to promote a more moderate understanding of Islam, emphasizing its teachings of peace and coexistence. Through this, they counteract extremist narratives that might appeal to their students.

These case studies underscore the versatility of educational approaches in the fight against radicalization. Each initiative is rooted in its unique cultural and geopolitical context, showcasing the need for tailored solutions. Yet, the common thread is evident – education, when applied carefully, can serve as a potent tool against extremism. The successes, challenges, and feedback from these programs offer invaluable lessons for nations and communities aiming to forge their own educational pathways against radicalization.

Chapter 22:
Lessons from History - Case Studies of Resolved Conflicts and Counter-terrorism Successes

As the ancient saying goes, "Those who cannot remember the past are condemned to repeat it." Drawing from this wisdom, history is replete with valuable lessons. We will explore a variety of cases where nations, communities, and individuals have successfully faced down the challenges posed by extremism. These lessons may be separated by geography, culture, and time, yet they all point to a common understanding: as formidable as it may seem, terrorism is not an unbeatable foe.

By examining historical case studies, we aim to unlock the secrets behind seemingly unsolvable conflicts, focusing on the methods, maneuvers, and means that eventually led to resolutions. From covert discussions in dark rooms to mass movements against destructive ideologies, these accounts spotlight the indomitable human drive for peace and stability. Our goal in scrutinizing these histories is not merely an academic endeavor; it is an aim to equip lawmakers, security professionals, and the public with the essential understanding and tools to shape a safer and more peaceful world. Though the journey to peace is rarely straightforward, the wisdom gleaned from past experiences often serves as a guiding light for the road ahead.

Historical Examples of Conflicts and Terrorism Successfully Resolved

Throughout history, numerous societies, ensnared in the grip of conflict and terrorism, have journeyed toward reconciliation and peace. Each narrative, distinct in its cultural, political, and geographical backdrop, weaves a broad array that offers optimism: even profound and enduring conflicts can witness resolution.

The Northern Ireland Troubles: Lasting from the late 1960s until the Good Friday Agreement in 1998, the Northern Ireland Troubles was a prolonged period of sectarian violence, civil unrest, and political deadlock between nationalist/republican and unionist/loyalist factions. The conflict was deeply rooted in historical, ethnic, and religious divides, with both sides resorting to armed conflict to pursue their goals.

Key to ending the impasse was the Good Friday Agreement, a monumental accomplishment reached after exhaustive negotiations that included not only the warring factions but also international mediators. The role of external facilitators, particularly from the United States, was crucial in brokering a deal that had long seemed impossible. These third parties brought fresh perspectives, neutrality, and leverage, all of which were vital in leading the opposing parties to the negotiating table and keeping them there. Furthermore, the years leading up to the agreement witnessed burgeoning grassroots movements advocating for peace. These initiatives, coupled with the war-weariness of the general populace, created an atmosphere conducive to dialogue and compromise.

The Good Friday Agreement stands as a testament to the efficacy of diplomatic dialogue and the importance of multilateral involvement. While not devoid of shortcomings and though tensions persist to some extent, the agreement dramatically reduced violence and laid the groundwork for a power-sharing government, proving that even deeply rooted conflicts can find resolution through sustained and inclusive dialogue. The lessons from Northern Ireland are particularly instructive for current and future policymakers, diplomats, and peace activists. They underline the need for creative diplomacy, the involvement of neutral mediators, and the powerful role public opinion can play in bringing about peace.

The Basque Struggle in Spain: Emerging in the late 1950s, the militant group ETA (Euskadi Ta Askatasuna) sought the independence of the Basque Country and engaged in various acts of terrorism, kidnappings, and political assassinations. Over the years, Spain's response to the ETA shifted from strict military interventions and repressive policing to more diplomatic strategies, including peace talks.

Central to the de-escalation of the conflict was a multifaceted approach that combined rigorous law enforcement actions with political dialogue. Spanish and French authorities collaborated to arrest key ETA leaders, significantly impacting the group's organizational structure and operational abilities. At the same time, Spain made attempts to negotiate, leading to several ceasefires, although these were temporary. Importantly, a change in the socio-political environment contributed to a decline in ETA activities. Over time, public support for ETA's violent methods dwindled, partly because of civil society movements that denounced violence and promoted peaceful coexistence. This societal shift was instrumental in compelling ETA to reconsider its tactics and ideology.

The culmination of these efforts was ETA's 2011 declaration of a "definitive cessation of its armed activity." This decision was not just the result of military or law enforcement pressure but also reflected a broader change in Basque and Spanish society that increasingly rejected violent methods. After decades of bloodshed, it was evident that a convergence of factors—consistent and effective law enforcement, public sentiment against violence, and open political dialogue—played a pivotal role in turning the tide.

This case provides valuable insights for decision-makers, security professionals, and academic researchers specializing in conflict resolution. It highlights the essential need for a multifaceted approach that goes beyond mere military intervention, incorporating diplomatic initiatives and community involvement as well.

The Sri Lankan Conflict with Tamil Tigers: Spanning 26 years from 1983 to 2009, the Sri Lankan civil war was an agonizing and relentless struggle between the Sri Lankan government and the Liberation Tigers of Tamil Eelam (LTTE), a separatist militant group with the goal of establishing an independent Tamil state in Sri Lanka's northern and eastern territories. Characterized by severe brutality, the conflict incorporated various violent tactics such as suicide bombings, guerrilla warfare, and targeted killings. The war had dire humanitarian consequences, displacing thousands who either became internally dislocated within Sri Lanka or sought refuge abroad, thereby triggering international relief efforts.

A turning point in the conflict came in the late 2000s when the Sri Lankan government embarked on an aggressive military campaign to finally defeat the LTTE. This was possible due to several factors. Firstly, international diplomatic engagement, especially by nations such as the United States, India, and several European countries, helped isolate the LTTE by designating it as a terrorist organization. This resulted in cutting off vital sources of funding and arms for the LTTE. Secondly, the Sri Lankan military underwent a series of transformations, including modernizing its arsenal and improving its tactics, which were instrumental in their ultimate victory. The government's adeptness in both land and naval warfare blocked LTTE's supply routes, gradually weakening the group's capabilities.

Another critical factor was the isolation of the LTTE, both financially and in terms of external support. Earlier in the conflict, the LTTE had significant backing in terms of financing from the Tamil diaspora and some foreign governments. However, as the conflict drew international attention and scrutiny, and as LTTE's tactics, including suicide bombings and attacks on civilians, were increasingly criticized, external support waned. This resulted in a drying up of crucial resources, rendering the LTTE more and more vulnerable to the Sri Lankan military's intensified campaign.

The case of the Sri Lankan conflict with the LTTE provides important lessons and cautions for conflict resolution. While the military defeat of the LTTE ended a significant armed conflict, it has not entirely resolved the underlying ethnic and political tensions that fueled the war in the first place. Therefore, while military and diplomatic strategies can be effective in the short term, addressing root causes is essential for lasting peace.

The Insurgency in Mozambique: The insurgency in Mozambique, largely seen as a byproduct of Cold War geopolitics and the aftermath of the nation's independence from Portugal in 1975, featured the ruling FRELIMO (Front for the Liberation of Mozambique) government pitted against the anti-communist faction RENAMO (Mozambican National Resistance). RENAMO's rebellion gained traction largely because of covert support from South Africa and, at times, Rhodesia (now Zimbabwe), as a way to counter communist influence in the region. The conflict was characterized by widespread atrocities, including forced recruitments, landmines, and the targeting of civilians, leading to a devastating humanitarian crisis.

Key to the eventual cessation of hostilities was the Rome General Peace Accords in 1992. This accord was not just a bilateral agreement between warring factions but a product of intense international mediation and collaboration. The involvement of global actors, particularly the Italian government and the Community of Sant'Egidio, a Catholic lay community, as neutral mediators was pivotal. These external parties provided a platform for dialogue, brokered trust, and even directly contributed to the content of the peace agreement. International observers and UN peacekeeping forces were involved in monitoring the ceasefire and demobilization efforts, lending further credence and stability to the peace process.

This case study underscores the vital role that international collaboration and neutral intermediation can play in resolving complex conflicts. It illustrates that domestic conflicts are often not isolated events but are deeply influenced by external geopolitical factors, and therefore, their resolution may also require international involvement. The role of neutral mediators proved to be essential in breaking the deadlock of distrust and in facilitating an agreement acceptable to all parties. It also demonstrates the importance of sustained engagement; international actors stayed involved during the sensitive post-accord period to oversee the successful implementation of the agreement. This multi-layered approach helped Mozambique transition from a war-torn nation to a country taking steps toward stability and democracy, albeit with ongoing challenges.

While each of these episodes varies in its specifics and resolutions, collectively, they highlight the diverse blend of elements required to navigate towards peace. Engagements at the diplomatic table, global interventions, civic initiatives, strategic military undertakings, and the unique timing of events all converge in the end. These past instances not only celebrate bygone successes but also provide invaluable insights for forthcoming endeavors in mitigating global terrorism and strife.

Strategies, Negotiations, and Policies that led to the Decline of Terrorist Organizations

The path to mitigating and ultimately neutralizing the risks associated with terrorist groups is complex, generally necessitating a blend of tactical operations, diplomatic engagements, and socio-political strategies. Studying the downfall of different extremist organizations provides a nuanced understanding of the effective measures, peace talks, and policies that played key roles in these successes.

Diplomatic Efforts: Diplomacy frequently serves as the front line in mitigating and solving complex conflicts involving terrorism or insurgencies. Its role is multifaceted, involving everything from facilitating dialogue to crafting international sanctions against entities supporting terrorism.

One prime example of diplomatic success can be seen in the 2016 peace agreement between the Colombian government and the Revolutionary Armed Forces of Colombia (FARC). This seminal agreement successfully concluded a long-standing conflict that had embroiled Colombia for more than 50 years, causing untold human and economic losses. The achievement was not the result of a quick or straightforward process, but of years of meticulous, often uncertain negotiations.

Of comment, numerous negotiations were not confined solely to the warring factions within Colombia. Several international parties, most prominently Cuba and Norway, acted as crucial mediators and hosts for the peace talks. Their neutral and stabilizing presence provided a secure and impartial environment in which both the Colombian government and FARC representatives could engage candidly. This international involvement lent an additional degree of credibility to the proceedings, creating a conducive atmosphere for both sides to consider and make the difficult, often painful, compromises that are the essence of any successful peace accord.

The Colombian example underscores the multifaceted role that diplomatic initiatives can play in resolving even the most stubborn of conflicts. Far beyond simply providing a forum for conversation, diplomatic endeavors can offer a structured, credible setting in which parties can air grievances, set forth conditions, and ultimately, arrive at mutually agreeable solutions. The outcome, though hard-won, serves as a testament to the idea that the path to lasting peace often lies through meticulous dialogue and negotiation, bolstered by international cooperation.

Peace Negotiations: Peace negotiations are a critical element in resolving conflicts, often serving as the culmination of diplomatic efforts and the gateway to long-term stability and reconciliation. While diplomatic dialogues set the stage for peace by opening lines of communication, formal negotiations allow warring parties to delve deeper into the root causes of conflicts and to craft comprehensive solutions.

A compelling illustration of the power of formal peace negotiations is the Dayton Agreement, which brought an end to the Bosnian War in 1995. This devastating conflict, a part of the larger Yugoslav Wars, involved ethnic and religious factions vying for control and led to significant loss of life and displacement. The negotiations, which took place in Dayton, Ohio, involved not only the primary belligerents—Bosnia and Herzegovina, Croatia, and Serbia—but were also mediated by the United States, European Union, and Russia.

These talks were a complex undertaking, addressing deeply rooted ethnic, territorial, and political issues. The involvement of international actors as mediators was indispensable in this scenario, as they were able to lend their expertise in conflict resolution and apply diplomatic pressure when necessary. While the talks were often fraught with tension and disagreement, the controlled environment allowed for productive dialogue that eventually led to a mutually agreeable path forward. One of the major achievements was the division of Bosnia and Herzegovina into two entities, the Federation of Bosnia and Herzegovina and the Republika (Republic of) Srpska, which allowed for a form of ethnic self-governance while still maintaining the country's territorial integrity.

What the Dayton Agreement underscores is the way formal negotiations can delve into the root causes of a conflict, offering nuanced solutions that go beyond immediate ceasefires or surface-level agreements. The structured negotiation process allowed for a systematic unpacking of complex grievances, territorial claims, and political aspirations, culminating in a detailed roadmap for the cessation of hostilities and a framework for future governance. By doing so, it transformed a volatile and seemingly intractable situation into a more stable and peaceful state of affairs, underlining the critical role that well-executed negotiations play in conflict resolution.

Security Measures: Alongside dialogue and negotiations, effective security strategies also play an essential role in achieving peace and resolving conflicts. One compelling example is the counter-insurgency campaign against the militant group Al-Shabaab in Somalia. Led by a coalition of African Union forces and supported by international partners, the operation sought to degrade the capabilities of Al-Shabaab, thereby reducing its influence and control over large swaths of territory. However, the military campaign was not a stand-alone effort; it was closely integrated with diplomatic initiatives and humanitarian aid to address the underlying issues of poverty and governance that contributed to the group's rise.

While military action may be necessary to neutralize immediate threats, it is crucial to employ such measures judiciously. This entails adhering to international laws and norms, including the minimization of civilian casualties and the strict observance of human rights. Any deviation from these principles could not only tarnish the reputation of the involved forces but also erode the local and international support that is often crucial for the success of a military campaign.

The implementation of security measures also involves intelligence gathering, logistics planning, and inter-agency coordination, among other factors. Counter-terrorism and counter-insurgency operations often run the risk of creating a vacuum of power or governance if not carefully planned and executed. Therefore, security strategies are usually most effective when they are part of a broader, multi-pronged approach that includes political, social, and economic initiatives to address the root causes of conflict.

International Collaboration: In a globalized world where challenges often cross borders, international collaboration becomes vital in addressing and combating transnational terrorism. A case in point is the international effort against ISIS (Islamic State of Iraq and Syria). The global coalition formed to counter ISIS included various nations contributing in different capacities—from military action to intelligence sharing and from economic sanctions to counter-propaganda efforts. By pooling resources and coordinating strategies, the coalition was able to degrade ISIS's military capabilities and significantly curtail its territorial gains.

This international collaboration went beyond military action; it extended to diplomatic and economic arenas as well. Several nations implemented strict sanctions and financial regulations to disrupt the flow of funds to ISIS, thus weakening its operational capabilities. Intelligence agencies from multiple countries shared information that led to the apprehension of key operatives and prevented numerous attacks. Non-governmental organizations and multilateral institutions worked to counteract the ideological appeal of extremist beliefs through education and public awareness campaigns.

The collective efforts effectively isolated ISIS, eroding its political and economic stability, and casting it as a pariah on the global stage. This case serves as a compelling illustration that addressing complex issues like terrorism calls for a multi-faceted, internationally coordinated response. By combining military, economic, diplomatic, and informational resources, nations stand a much better chance of neutralizing threats and ensuring global security. Therefore, the international community must continue to foster such collaborations to adapt and respond to evolving global challenges.

Policy Reforms: Tackling the root causes of terrorism requires an approach that goes beyond military and intelligence operations. Governments must engage in proactive policy reforms that aim to address the underlying issues fueling radicalization and extremism. Factors like socioeconomic disparities, political disenfranchisement, and cultural marginalization often serve as catalysts for individuals to gravitate towards extremist ideologies.

For instance, initiatives that focus on education and job creation in impoverished areas can significantly mitigate the allure of extremist groups, which often promises financial security to recruits. By improving access to quality education, governments can empower young people with the tools they need for economic self-sufficiency and social mobility, thus making the propaganda of extremist groups less appealing. Similarly, robust social welfare programs can provide a safety net for those who might otherwise feel compelled to join extremist organizations out of economic desperation.

Additionally, political reforms aimed at fostering inclusivity can also play a key role in prevention. Marginalized communities are less likely to turn to extremism if they feel that they have a voice in the political process and that their grievances can be addressed through legitimate means. Measures such as electoral reform, anti-discrimination laws, and community engagement initiatives can go a long way in building trust and encouraging participation in democratic processes.

Lastly, cultural initiatives aimed at promoting social cohesion can also contribute to prevention efforts. Public awareness campaigns, educational programs, and community events that celebrate diversity and promote understanding among different ethnic, religious, and social groups can counteract the divisive narratives propagated by extremist organizations.

Grassroots Movements: Sometimes the most powerful catalysts for change emerge from the ground up, rather than trickling down from governments or international organizations. Grassroots movements, marked by community dialogues, civic activism, and the collective sentiment of a populace weary of conflict, can profoundly shift the dynamics of entrenched struggles. Such movements not only reveal the human costs of conflict but also offer alternative narratives and solutions that might be overlooked at the national or international level.

For example, local peace-building initiatives may organize community dialogues that bring together individuals from opposing sides of a conflict to share their stories, discuss their grievances, and explore possible avenues for cooperation. These dialogues can dismantle stereotypes, build empathy, and foster a sense of common humanity that is often lost in the heat of conflict. The influence of such dialogues can radiate outward, affecting public opinion and putting pressure on leaders to seek peaceful solutions.

Public sentiment, galvanized through awareness campaigns, protests, or social media, can also compel action. In several instances, large-scale peaceful protests have effectively pressured governments to reevaluate their strategies, reconsider the use of force, and engage in negotiations with opposing factions. Moreover, a populace well-informed about the complexities and costs of ongoing conflict can act as a significant check on the escalation of violence, demanding accountability and transparency from their leaders.

Another avenue through which grassroots movements can be effective is in bridging the gap between policy and implementation. Often, international agreements or government policies falter in the execution phase due to a lack of community engagement. Grassroots organizations can step in to facilitate this, ensuring that peace agreements are not just signed but are also meaningfully implemented at the community level.

Lastly, grassroots movements often catch the attention of international organizations and foreign governments, influencing diplomatic efforts and even contributing to the mobilization of international aid and resources. They help to humanize abstract political issues, drawing attention to the on-the-ground realities and needs, thus affecting policy both domestically and internationally.

Applying Historical Insights to Contemporary Challenges

History serves as an invaluable repository of insights for contemporary challenges in counter-terrorism. While the context and players change, certain fundamental principles remain constant, and the successes of the past offer a roadmap to navigate the complexities of today's threats.

Combatting Ideological Extremism: Historical successes, such as the quelling of radical ideologies during the Cold War, teach us the value of countering propaganda with strategic information campaigns. Modern extremist ideologies, proliferated through the internet and social media, can be countered by leveraging technology to promote narratives of unity, peace, and mutual respect. Further, grassroots community engagement, as practiced during the aftermath of internal conflicts in nations like Rwanda, can be instrumental in preventing radicalization at its roots.

Addressing Separatist Movements: Many separatist movements, such as the IRA in Northern Ireland, were pacified through inclusive dialogues and ensuring political representation. In contemporary contexts, ensuring that marginalized communities have a voice in governance can mitigate feelings of disenfranchisement and reduce the allure of violent separatism.
Engaging in Multilateral Diplomacy: The resolutions of several 20th-century conflicts, like the Camp David Accords between Egypt and Israel, underscored the importance of multilateral diplomacy. As modern terrorism and conflicts often transcend borders, engaging in international collaborations and peacekeeping initiatives can prove pivotal.

Leveraging Intelligence Networks: The decline of many extremist movements in the past was hastened by efficient intelligence operations. With the rise of digital technologies, there is an opportunity to build on this historical wisdom by fostering international intelligence sharing, employing big data analytics, and developing cybersecurity measures.

Balancing Security and Civil Liberties: Historically, efforts that disproportionately restricted civil liberties in the name of security often backfired, giving rise to resentment and further radicalization. The challenge today lies in employing surveillance and security measures without infringing on individual rights, ensuring that the counter-terrorism measures themselves do not become a catalyst for discontent.

Rehabilitation and Reintegration: Successful disarmament, demobilization, and reintegration (DDR) programs, as seen in post-conflict regions like Sierra Leone, emphasize the need for rehabilitating radicals. Contemporary counter-terrorism efforts can benefit from establishing deradicalization programs, focusing on education, counseling, and reintegrating former extremists into society.

By blending historical wisdom with an understanding of modern distinctions, policymakers and security experts can craft strategies that are both grounded and innovative. This synergy between past and present not only enhances counter-terrorism approaches but also improves the prospects of building a more peaceful future.

Chapter 23:
Future Trends in Terrorism - Emerging Threats and Responses

In the ever-shifting global landscape, terrorism continues to adapt, leveraging new tools, technologies, and tactics to achieve its aims. This adaptation prompts a necessity for counter-terrorism measures to be equally dynamic and forward-thinking. As we venture into the future, discerning the trends that could potentially define the next intervals of extremism is paramount. Advanced technologies such as artificial intelligence, biotechnology, and cyber capabilities could offer terrorists a broader palette for destruction. There is potential for drones to be used for precise attacks, while genetic engineering might find its dark side in bioterrorism. Simultaneously, the obscurity of the dark web could provide extremist groups the space they need for recruitment, planning, and generating funds.

Furthermore, the structure of terrorist organizations is undergoing transformation. Traditional hierarchies may soon be replaced by more fluid, decentralized networks, made possible by the broad reach of social media. Such decentralized formations could prove more challenging to track for intelligence agencies, as they might lack a clear central leadership to target. As the perceptions of global climate crises continues to grow, we may also witness a rise in eco-terrorism, where extremist factions target those they perceive as culprits of environmental degradation. Resource shortages may further ignite regional conflicts, adding another dimension to terrorist activities. Ideologies, too, are not static. While historical acts of terror have often been motivated by religious or political beliefs, future extremists might find their rallying cries in causes like technological singularity, anti-globalization, lack of freedoms, or even extreme forms of nativism.

Reacting to this fluid threat landscape requires a multi-layered approach. Enhanced global collaboration, underpinned by international intelligence-sharing, will be crucial in stemming the tide of terrorism. Similarly, technological advancements should be harnessed for defense, with AI-driven surveillance, cybersecurity measures, and predictive analytics serving as bulwarks against extremist actions. As threats diversify, there is an urgent need to bolster our infrastructure to resist varied attack forms. Furthermore, public awareness campaigns can serve as early warning systems, making populations vigilant and prepared.

Lastly, and perhaps most crucially, addressing the root causes of radicalization, whether they stem from socio-economic disparities, political exclusion, or other forms of grievances, will be central to any comprehensive counter-terrorism strategy. In navigating the uncertain pathways of the future, it is vital to recognize and prepare for these shifts in terrorism's landscape, ensuring that our defensive strategies evolve in tandem with the challenges they confront.

Technological Advancements and Their Impact on Terrorism

In the modern era, technological advancements have unfurled at an unprecedented pace, introducing a plethora of tools and platforms that, while designed for progress, can also be manipulated for malevolent purposes. As these cutting-edge technologies continue to emerge, terrorist groups have shown adaptability, exploring new means to further their agendas.

Take, for instance, AI. While AI can revolutionize industries and improve quality of life, in the hands of extremists, it has the potential to disrupt intelligence operations or be used to manipulate public opinion. Propaganda can be tailor-made using AI algorithms to target susceptible individuals, making radicalization more efficient. Deepfake technologies, powered by AI, can generate convincing yet entirely fictitious content, sowing discord and mistrust among communities or even nations.

Drones, which were initially designed for surveillance and recreation, have also been weaponized by terrorists. Their ability to carry payloads means they can be used for precision attacks on strategic targets, evading traditional security measures. With drones, terrorists can strike from a distance, reducing their risk of capture or retaliation.

Biotechnology, a frontier that promises to revolutionize healthcare, also presents a double-edged sword. The same techniques that allow for the manipulation of genes for medical purposes could be used malevolently to engineer pathogens, leading to a new age of bioterrorism. By manipulating or creating viruses and bacteria, terrorists could unleash pandemics, creating chaos, fear, and immense human suffering.

Moreover, the digital landscape, characterized by the dark web, offers terrorists anonymity. Here, they can communicate, recruit, plan, and even fundraise without leaving much of a trace. Cryptocurrencies, decentralized and difficult to track, offer new avenues for financing illicit activities, bypassing traditional banking systems.

Understanding the evolving technological landscape is thus crucial in the fight against terrorism. As these technologies continue to advance, they will invariably alter the tactics and strategies employed by terrorist groups. The challenge for counter-terrorism agencies is twofold: to stay ahead in this technological arms race and to harness these very technologies as tools to counteract and prevent terrorist activities.

Biological and Chemical Threats: Possibilities and Preparedness

The concept of biological and chemical warfare has historically been relegated to the annals of large-scale military conflict. Yet, in a world where extremist ideologies intersect with accessible knowledge, the potential for terrorists to harness these agents as weapons of terror is becoming an alarming reality. Bioterrorism, using biological agents such as bacteria, viruses, or toxins, and chemical terrorism, involving hazardous chemicals, can wreak havoc not just through immediate casualties, but by inciting widespread panic and overwhelming healthcare systems.

Bioterrorism poses a unique and multifaceted threat. Simple to disseminate and hard to detect, a well-executed biological attack could lead to large-scale outbreaks of diseases, some of which might be rare or eradicated, thereby catching public health systems off guard. The challenge is further compounded by the possibility of terrorists using genetic engineering to create more potent or drug-resistant strains of pathogens.

Chemical threats, on the other hand, offer immediacy. A chemical release in an urban setting, be it through contamination of water supplies or aerial dispersion, can lead to instantaneous casualties, disrupt communities, and pose daunting challenges for emergency responders.

Recognizing these threats, governments and international organizations have been bolstering their defenses. Advanced detection systems are being deployed at transportation hubs and critical infrastructure to identify and warn of these threats early. Research labs across the world are working on broad-spectrum antivirals and antidotes to counter potential biological and chemical agents. Public health agencies are creating stockpiles of vaccines, antibiotics, and antitoxins to ensure swift medical responses. Moreover, drills simulating bioterrorism and chemical attack scenarios are becoming commonplace, aiming to train emergency responders and healthcare professionals in effective crisis management.

Equally crucial is the global effort to curb the proliferation of these agents. International conventions and agreements, such as the Biological Weapons Convention (BWC) and the Chemical Weapons Convention (CWC), aim to restrict the production and stockpiling of biological and chemical weapons.

In a landscape where terror threats are evolving, understanding the menace of biological and chemical terrorism, along with investing in preparedness and countermeasures, is paramount to safeguarding global security and public health.

Space, Cyber, and Quantum Terrorism: Imagining the Unthinkable

The constantly evolving technological landscape, while bringing about unprecedented advancements, also unveils new dimensions for potential threats. One need only cast their gaze upwards to understand the significance of space in the contemporary world. Satellites orbiting our planet play an integral role in everything from communication and navigation to global defense systems. The deliberate targeting or sabotage of these satellites by terrorists could disrupt these services, causing not only strategic havoc but potential real-world chaos — imagine air traffic systems going haywire or crucial defense satellites going offline during a crisis.

Closer to home, the digital realm poses arguably the most immediate threat. Cyberterrorism is not just a plotline for modern thrillers; it is an emergent reality. Critical infrastructure, including power grids, water supplies, and healthcare systems, relies heavily on interconnected networks. A coordinated cyber-attack could cripple these systems, plunging cities into darkness, disrupting essential services, or even causing direct harm, such as tampering with a city's water supply. The potential fallout from such attacks is not merely physical; the psychological and economic ramifications could be equally profound, with public confidence in systems and services severely shaken.

Yet, as quantum computing gradually transitions from theoretical physics to practical application, it opens the door to a new frontier of threats: quantum terrorism. Though in its infancy, quantum computing promises computational power that dwarfs our current capabilities. In the wrong hands, such power could be used to break conventional encryption methods, making previously secure data vulnerable. More speculatively, as quantum technologies evolve, they might enable new methods of attack or disruption that we have not even conceived of yet.

But it is not all doom and gloom. With the recognition of these potential threats comes a determination to fortify against them. Space treaties and conventions are being re-evaluated to ensure the security of outer space assets. Governments and private sectors worldwide are investing billions into cybersecurity, developing more robust defenses and rapid response capabilities. And as quantum technologies evolve, so too will the security protocols designed to protect them.

The journey into these new technological frontiers demands vigilance. While we marvel at the possibilities they offer, we must also remain aware of the new vulnerabilities they introduce. By understanding and anticipating these challenges, we can hope to safeguard the promise of tomorrow from the threats of today.

Proactive Approaches: Anticipating and Mitigating Future Threats

In the fast-paced, constantly evolving landscape of global security, the adage "forewarned is forearmed" holds true now more than ever. While we cannot predict the future with certainty, understanding potential threats and taking a proactive stance can mean the difference between prevention and catastrophe.

One of the cornerstones of proactive defense is forward-looking intelligence. This does not merely involve gathering data but also analyzing it to identify patterns, discerning underlying motives, and forecasting possible trajectories. It is an art as much as it is a science, blending cutting-edge technology with the age-old skills of human intuition and analysis.

Scenario planning is another vital tool in the counter-terrorism toolkit. By envisioning a range of possible futures, from the most likely to the most deadly-case scenario, policymakers and strategists can craft a multiplicity of responses. This sort of planning is not about prediction; it is about preparation. It enables swift and decisive action in the face of unfolding events, minimizing reactionary delays.

Risk assessment, meanwhile, forms the bedrock of our defenses against emerging threats. It is a meticulous process of evaluating vulnerabilities, determining the likelihood of different threat vectors, and weighing potential impacts. Through risk assessment, resources can be allocated more effectively, protective measures can be bolstered where they are weakest, and strategies can be adapted to the ever-shifting threat landscape.

Governments, intelligence agencies, and security organizations around the world are increasingly recognizing the importance of these proactive approaches. Whether through investing in next-gen surveillance technologies, collaborating with international counterparts for wider intelligence networks, or engaging in war games and simulation exercises to test preparedness, they are working relentlessly to remain a step ahead of potential adversaries.

Ultimately, the goal is clear: to anticipate, adapt, and act before threats fully materialize. In an age where the nature of threats is constantly in flux, agility, foresight, and collaboration will be the keys to safeguarding our future.

Ethical and Legal Considerations in Addressing Future Terrorism

The fast-paced evolution of technology and tactics in the realm of terrorism poses significant ethical and legal challenges. While advancements offer unparalleled capabilities for monitoring, detection, and response, they also introduce moral dilemmas and potential legal pitfalls.

Drones, for instance, have transformed the landscape of counter-terrorism operations. Their ability to surveil vast areas and execute targeted strikes has rendered them indispensable. Yet, their use raises complex ethical questions. The specter of remote warfare, where decisions about life and death are made thousands of miles away from the battlefield, challenges traditional notions of combat ethics. Civilian casualties, issues of proportionality, and the very notion of "targeted killings" are under intense scrutiny. Legally, the use of drones in sovereign territories without explicit consent introduces concerns about violation of international law.

Cyberterrorism, meanwhile, is a relatively new frontier but one that holds profound implications. Responding to cyber threats can be especially challenging, given the amorphous nature of the internet and the ease with which cyber-terrorists can conceal their identities and locations. While it is imperative to protect critical infrastructures and maintain national security, the methods used to monitor, detect, and counter cyber threats can infringe upon privacy rights. The act of attributing a cyber-attack to a particular actor or nation and retaliating has its own set of legal implications.

Moreover, as governments ramp up surveillance and data collection to preempt threats, the inevitable tension between security imperatives and civil liberties surfaces. The line between safeguarding the public and infringing upon individual rights becomes blurred. Surveillance measures, while essential for security, can, if unchecked, venture into the realm of overreach, eroding the very democratic values they aim to protect.

As we navigate this intricate landscape, open dialogues are crucial. Engaging ethicists, legal scholars, policymakers, and the public in discussions ensures that our approach to address future acts of terrorism is not only effective but also grounded in our shared values. Balancing the need for security with the upholding of civil liberties and international law will be central to these endeavors. After all, in countering terrorism, it is not just about the threats we face but the kind of society we aspire to be.

Conclusion:
Navigating the Labyrinth of Terrorism in a Globalized World

In the pages of this book, readers have undertaken an expansive journey, dissecting the multifaceted nature of terrorism. From its inception as isolated acts of political violence to its evolution into sophisticated, globally-networked enterprises, terrorism's capacity to adapt and evolve in tandem with global shifts has been laid bare. By closely examining its historical trajectory, one discerns the flexibility of terrorist strategies, which have continually redefined themselves in the face of changing societal, technological, and political landscapes. This adaptability, while being the cornerstone of its persistence, also epitomizes the complexities encountered by those in the vanguard against it.

A deeper examination brings to the fore the intricate dance between socio-economic factors and the lure of extremist ideologies. Even though poverty, illiteracy, and stark economic disparities do not directly produce terrorists, these conditions often create fertile grounds where extremist narratives can take root and flourish. It is imperative, therefore, that counter-terrorism strategies incorporate initiatives that target these underlying vulnerabilities. By investing in education, economic empowerment, and social equity, the battle against terrorism is waged not just on the frontlines but at its very roots.

Our foray into the digital realm has exposed the transformative, yet ambivalent, role of technology. The internet, with its boundless horizons, offers extremist groups a powerful amplifier for their propaganda, a ubiquitous platform for recruitment, and an intricate expanse for coordination. However, this same digital realm offers governments and counter-terrorism agencies unprecedented tools—real-time surveillance, data analytics, and the dissemination of counter-narratives, to name a few. The challenge lies in harnessing this digital arsenal without compromising the very values—freedom, privacy, and democracy—that we seek to protect.
Central to our discourse is the realization of the profound impact of collaborative efforts.

Terrorism, with its tentacles stretching across continents, requires a response that is equally global in its scope. Nations must set aside historical rivalries, political differences, and economic competitions to unite against this shared menace. Joint intelligence ventures, synchronized military operations, shared best practices, and aligned socio-economic initiatives form the bulwark of this united front.

Gazing into the horizon, it is abundantly clear that the confrontation with terrorism is a protracted one, demanding not just superior firepower, but the power of ideas, shared narratives, and an unwavering global commitment. This commitment manifests as a vision of a world where grievances find expression not in violence, but in dialogues; where diverse faiths, cultures, and ideologies are celebrated as enriching tapestries rather than divisive chasms. The road ahead, though fraught with challenges, is not insurmountable. Bolstered by humanity's storied resilience, driven by understanding and fortified by global cooperation, we are poised to navigate and ultimately transcend the intricate maze of terrorism in this interconnected world.

Appendices

A: Notable Terrorist Attacks Throughout History

1. May 7, 1968 - University of Valle Bombing, Colombia
2. June 27, 1976 - Air France Flight 139 Hijacking, Entebbe, Uganda
3. April 18, 1983 - U.S. Embassy Bombing in Beirut, Lebanon
4. December 12, 1985 - Arrow Air Flight 1285 Crash, Canada
5. March 12, 1993 - Bombay Bombings, India
6. February 15, 1996 - Sri Lanka Central Bank Bombing
7. July 25, 2000 - Air France Flight 4590 Crash, France
8. March 11, 2002 - Passover Massacre, Israel
9. September 20, 2008 - Islamabad Marriott Hotel Bombing, Pakistan
10. January 27, 2011 - Moscow International Airport Bombing, Russia
11. May 11, 2011 - Monterrey Casino Attack, Mexico
12. May 22, 2013 - Woolwich Attack, United Kingdom
13. January 9, 2015 - Hypercacher Kosher Supermarket Siege, France
14. March 20, 2015 - Sanaa Mosque Bombings, Yemen
15. June 17, 2015 - Charleston Church Shooting, United States
16. August 17, 2015 - Bangkok Shrine Bombing, Thailand
17. January 15, 2016 - Ouagadougou Attacks, Burkina Faso
18. December 19, 2016 - Berlin Christmas Market Attack, Germany
19. April 3, 2017 - Saint Petersburg Metro Bombing, Russia
20. August 12, 2017 - Charlottesville Car Attack, United States
21. October 1, 2017 - Las Vegas Shooting, United States
22. October 14, 2017 - Mogadishu Bombings, Somalia
23. November 29, 2017 - Sinai Mosque Attack, Egypt
24. October 17, 2018 - Kerch Polytechnic College Attack, Crimea, Russia
25. March 15, 2019 - Christchurch Mosque Shootings, New Zealand
26. June 18, 2019 - Kabul Bombing, Afghanistan
27. August 3, 2019 - El Paso Shooting, United States
28. November 29, 2019 - London Bridge Stabbing, United Kingdom
29. December 29, 2019 - Texas Church Shooting, United States
30. May 12, 2020 - Kabul Maternity Ward Attack, Afghanistan
31. January 30, 2020 - Philippines Church Bombing
32. January 2, 2021 - Twin Suicide Bombing in Baghdad, Iraq
33. March 20, 2021 - Palma Attack, Mozambique
34. August 26, 2021 - Kabul Airport Bombings, Afghanistan
35. September 3, 2021 - New Zealand Supermarket Stabbing

This list, while extensive, still only covers a portion of notable terrorist attacks throughout history, underscoring the global and persistent nature of the threat of terrorism.

B: Counter-terrorism Agencies Around the World

1. United States: Federal Bureau of Investigation (FBI) - Counter-terrorism Division, and Central Intelligence Agency (CIA) - Counterterrorist Center.
2. United Kingdom: MI5 - The Security Service, and Counter Terrorism Command (SO15).
3. Russia: Federal Security Service (FSB) and Special Purpose Mobility Unit (OMON).
4. India: National Investigation Agency (NIA) and Research and Analysis Wing (R&AW).
5. Israel: Shin Bet (Israel Security Agency) and Mossad's Metsada unit.
6. France: Directorate General for External Security (DGSE) and Central Directorate of Interior Intelligence (DCRI).
7. Australia: Australian Security Intelligence Organization (ASIO) and Joint Counter Terrorism Teams (JCTT).
8. Germany: Federal Office for the Protection of the Constitution (BfV) and Federal Criminal Police Office (BKA) - Counter-Terrorism Section.
9. Canada: Canadian Security Intelligence Service (CSIS) and Integrated National Security Enforcement Teams (INSET).
10. Pakistan: Inter-Services Intelligence (ISI) - Counter-Intelligence wing and Counter Terrorism Department (CTD) of the Police.
11. China: Ministry of State Security (MSS) and People's Armed Police (PAP) - Counter-terrorism units.
12. Italy: Central Directorate for Anti-Terrorism Police (DAP) and Carabinieri Special Intervention Group (GIS).
13. Spain: Centro Nacional de Inteligencia (CNI) and Special Group for Counter-Terrorist Warfare (GEO).
14. Japan: Public Security Intelligence Agency (PSIA) and Counter Terrorism Unit of the Tokyo Metropolitan Police Department.
15. Brazil: Brazilian Intelligence Agency (ABIN) and Federal Police - Anti-Terrorism Division.
16. Saudi Arabia: General Intelligence Presidency (GIP) and Special Emergency Forces (SEF).
17. Egypt: General Intelligence Directorate (GID) and National Security Service.
18. South Africa: State Security Agency (SSA) and Directorate for Priority Crime Investigation (Hawks) - Counter-terrorism unit.
19. Indonesia: Badan Intelijen Negara (BIN) and Detachment 88 - an elite counter-terrorism police squad.
20. Turkey: National Intelligence Organization (MIT) and Police Special Operation Department.

A Note of Thanks to You, the Reader

Dear Reader,

I would like this opportunity to express my sincere gratitude for your willingness to join me on this journey through the complex subjects of terrorism and counter-terrorism. I am also truly thankful for your commitment to expand your mind on such intricate issues.

This book aims not just to illuminate the subjects of terrorism and counter-terrorism, but also to highlight the transformative power of understanding, open dialogue, and collective action. My hope is that you have found enlightenment within these pages, encountered provocative questions, and perhaps even felt inspired to delve deeper into the subject matter.

Books are, at their core, a collaborative conversation between the author, the subject, and you – the reader. Thank you for enriching this dialogue through your curiosity, compassion, and quest to understand the complexities of our world.

In an era, rife with change and uncertainty, insightful and engaged readers like you serve as beacons of hope. Through greater understanding, we can aspire to build bridges, nurture peace, and cultivate a world that celebrates both its differences and its shared human experience.

Once again, thank you for being a part of this journey. May your future be guided by wisdom, empathy, and an unwavering faith in the potential for a better tomorrow.

Warmly,

Andrew Weaver